Misadventure, Mayhem, Myth and Murder

The Dark Side of Axholme's Past

by Robert E. Fish

Published jointly by Haywood Books Ltd and JJMoffs Independent Book Publisher Ltd 2018

Copyright ©Robert E. Fish 2018

All rights reserved.
No part of this publication may be reproduced, stored in a retrieval system or transmitted in any form or by any means, without the prior permission in writing of the publisher. Neither may it be otherwise circulated in any form of binding or cover other than that in which it is published and without a similar condition including this condition being imposed on the subsequent purchaser.

Robert E. Fish has asserted his right under The Copyright, Designs and Patents Act, 1988 to be identified as the author of this work.

Haywood Books Ltd, 7 Burnham Road, Epworth, North Lincolnshire and
JJMoffs Independent Book Publisher Ltd, Grove House Farm,
Grovewood Road, Misterton, Nottinghamshire, DN10 4EF.

Typeset and cover design by Anna Richards

Contents

1	The Isle of Axholme
4	Ware Aegir
23	Customs
33	Danger on the Highway
48	Hazards from Above
61	Moorland Myths
81	Riot
92	Home Medicine, Quackery and Alchemy
100	Death on the Tracks
110	What's Your Poison
116	Temporary Insanity
128	Fire and Flame
140	Grave Mistakes and a Turbulent Priest
149	In Cold Blood
156	Found Drowned
163	They are in Heaven
173	Good Cop, Bad Cop
182	Threats to Health and a Close Shave
188	A Novel Mystery
192	One War after Another

INTRODUCTION

The Isle of Axholme

In the extreme north-west of the county of Lincolnshire lies an area of land known as The Isle of Axholme. The name Isle was given to the area long before the Dutch drainage engineer Cornelius Vermuyden arrived in the 1620s to divert the waters and reclaim the land. Etymological studies confirm that Axholme means island by Haxey, combining an Isle town name with the Old Norse word holmr meaning island. Interestingly, the Old English suffix 'ey' in Haxey also refers to 'island.' So we are left with the intriguing prospect of the Isle of Axholme being the island of an island's island!

The area has three small towns: Epworth, Crowle and the previously mentioned Haxey, along with the communities of Althorpe, Amcotts, Beltoft, Belton, Burnham (High and Low), Derrythorpe, East Lound, Eastoft, Garthorpe, Graiselound, Gunthorpe, Keadby, Luddington, Owston Ferry, Sandtoft, West Butterwick, Westwoodside, and Wroot. The major settlements were built on areas of dry, raised ground in the surrounding marshland, binding themselves to the more elevated, central spine that runs along a north/south axis. On the low lying areas are the smaller settlements and the wild Turbaries of Haxey, Epworth and Belton and the Moors of Crowle. In the northern half of Axholme lie the remains of two deserted medieval villages, Haldenby and Waterton.

Although geographically separated from the rest of Lincolnshire by the 'mighty' Trent, Axholme still retains some of the county's unique cultural traditions. However, its proximity to Yorkshire and

Nottinghamshire has enriched further the Isle's heritage, folklore and historical conventions. Paradoxically, Axholme is more attuned to the Humberhead area of Hatfield Chase and Goole Fields and the Nottinghamshire district of Bassetlaw than it is to its mother county. Characterised by flood defence and land improvement, modern-day Axholme owes much to the reclamation schemes begun in the Middle Ages, the considerable, but much-maligned work of Cornelius Vermuyden and the finer tuning of John Smeaton in the mid-1700s for the high status of its heritage and agricultural output.

Post-conquest Axholme was a dismal place, populated in the main by fish, waterfowl and rats. Here and there, the hut of a fowler or a peat stack, raised for fuel by those who lived on the higher ground, broke the skyline of the reedy morass. The whole place was a festering landscape; a rank moorland of quaking bogs and treacherous, green-scummed mire-pits that bred agues and fever and fostered in the locals, suspicion and hostility. The occupants traversed the wastes along narrow tracks, stalked the watery wastes on stilts and sailed across the meres in their flat-bottomed boats. They carried poles to thrust into the ground to determine the depth of the mire. In places, these poles could 'disappear' up to ten, twelve, or even fifteen feet leaving the holder grateful that it was the pole disappearing and not them!

True Islonians are proud of their history and, though strictly not an island any longer, speak of living 'on the Isle.' Axholme was, in fact, a series of islands, a small archipelago above an inhospitable marshland with a cluster of ferry settlements by the riverbanks. The arrival of the Vermuyden, however, set a pivot in the timeline of Axholme's history. When speaking of the Isle, locals, and historians readily reference the time as 'before' or 'after' the drainage. In truth, the turbulence this brought to the area did not define Axholme's stubborn character, for it was already so, being born from the savage ruthlessness of isolated living. However, Vermuyden's ill-conceived scheme provided another conduit for the locals' malign attitude toward those who 'came in from outside.' Seeing their livelihood under threat roused Axholme folk to a 'spiteful spirit' and exemplified a cohesive disdain for authority that remains to this day. In truth, these Island folk had little concept of the lack of political understanding held by 'Vermuyden's immigrants' who came to Axholme looking for a better life – they were foreigners and, as such, not deserving of kindness. If they wouldn't leave voluntarily, then they would have to be driven out.

While researching my previous book on the History of Epworth I came across stories cataloguing what one can only describe as the darker side of Axholme's past. In the local newspapers and embedded in folklore were stories of suffering caused by ignorance and isolation; of violence fueled by perceived wrong or by greed and envy; of addiction to alcohol and drugs, and of suicides, careless accidents, and murder.

I have not set out to sensationalise or trivialise these stories from the past but to place them in the context of the social norms that existed at the time. Some may seem at odds with modern living, but they come from a time when mental health problems were judged to arise from an invasive evil; when medical ignorance rendered human life 'cheap' and when, for many, superstition directed everyday life. If this makes you uneasy dear reader then, this book, which explores the faults and flaws of the people of Axholme, is not for you. If, like me, however, your interest lies in exploring the complexities, inner turmoils, and tragedies that, until they happen, sit behind what many of us term 'normality,' then read on!

CHAPTER ONE

'Ware Aegir'

MISADVENTURE

The River Trent marks the eastern boundary of the Isle of Axholme. One time master of the Isle (along with its co-conspirator rivers, the Torne, the Idle and the Don) it has accepted enslavement reluctantly. Long recognised as an unpredictable, even capricious river, over the years, the spread of its malevolent waters across the land has brought profit, productivity, adversity and grief to those who've lived within its reach. Claimed by many to be the 'Highway to the Sea,' it was said if you could navigate the Trent you could navigate any river in the world. A channel for trade and travel since ancient times, during the Roman Occupation, their galley boats would navigate the route from Boston to York on what was known as 'The Grain Run.' The river, which fed and received water from the rapacious gullet of the River Humber was the main route inland for many Germanic and Norse tribes, and these have left their mark in the name of settlements with the suffix 'thorpe' along the Axholme section.

By Domesday, the river was considered significant enough to warrant the threat of fines against anyone who impeded boats along its navigable course. In the late medieval period, the river was alive with fishing weirs and mills, ferries, fords and bridges and by the nineteenth century, a series of Acts of Parliament further sought to better regulate river trade. Bargee Thomas Spick, who worked on Trent cargo ketches throughout the nineteenth century, spoke of fleets of boats carrying grain from Hull to Nottingham and returning loaded with coal. Spick likened the river 'to many of

Residents on South Street, Owston Ferry attempt to hold back the flooding River Trent

nature's phenomenon that needed the skill and labour of man to exploit its potential and release its benefits, and a fortitude of spirit to deal with its destructive impact.'

In more recent times, the river, encased by banks and levees has bent to the will of man. Too big to be tamed fully, however, it still exerts a malign influence over the surrounding land. A place to avoid for many, even those who appreciate its ever-present danger find themselves drawn to its shifting moods. All along its Axholme banks, a familiar sight is that of locals stood, or sat, staring out across the water, as though hypnotised by its mesmeric swirls and eddies. In days gone by, when the ice of severe winters halted the river's progress, locals carried brushwood and braziers onto the frozen mass and, having roasted a bullock, tucked into a warming meal. They followed this with social and competitive skating events. In times of flood, those who lived 'on the Trentside' had little defence against the onrushing water. They stored buckets of clay, sandbags and damp boards in their backyards ready to defend their homes against the inrushing water. When these proved inadequate, families hauled carpets and furniture upstairs, and, having opened the front door to let in the water would open the back door to let it out! After a few days living like this and, having allowed the floor to dry out, the family would move back down until the next 'event.'

Heavy gales and storms in the North Sea in November 1928 saw an exceptionally high tide sweep up the Trent, taking villagers and farmers by surprise. In Owston Ferry, the water overflowed as far as the recreation field, half a mile from the river.

A flooded Market Place - Owston Ferry

At its worst, children had to be carried to school through the thigh-high water on the shoulders of their parents, and farmers waded to their pig sties to rescue their animals in a like manner. Small items of furniture and domestic utensils could be seen floating in the Market Place and along the riverside streets, beer barrels floated in the cellar of the White Hart Hotel and fleets of haystacks made a curious sight as they 'sailed' away in the currents; the smaller ones whirling round in the eddying water while the larger ones made their way forward in a more stately manner. The height and force of the water floated off the doors of the jetty traps adding to the hazard. Residents deployed rowing boats intended for use on the river, to help them and others maintain a semblance of daily life. When the waters subsided, rather than attempt to clear up the mess, workmen began erecting barricades along the banks in preparation for the next high tide.

'Ware Aegir' - the tidal bore passes Kelfield in the 1950s

Regarded by many as a necessary evil, those who worked on the river for a living, found the disruption an acceptable price to pay. For them, ease of access to Hull and the trade this created, brought prosperity and employment.

Although much of the Trent's route is quiet and remote, the stage through Axholme is, perhaps, the most mysterious and foreboding. It is here that the lunging tidal bore, the Aegir, is at its most potent. This wave, which some say takes its name from Aegir, the Norse god of the ocean, occurs when a spring tide enters the funnel shape of the river mouth and the salt water tide pushes back on the flow of fresh water, turning the river's broad channel into frothing energy. Others counter this argument and say the name derives from the Old English word 'hygre' (originally applied to other tidal bores such as that on the River Severn well away from

Norse influence). When conditions are right, this tidal bore can reach heights of six feet. When such a huge wave rushes up a superficially placid river, is there little wonder our ancestors saw it as a supernatural occurrence?

South of Gainsborough where the once powerful Aegir becomes little more than a ripple, legend has it that here King Canute, knowing the bore would recede, claimed he could halt the tide. Caricatured as a fool for thinking something so absurd, another version of the story paints the now Christian Canute in an altogether different light. Carried on his throne to the river's edge as the Aegir came towards him, he called out for it to stop but, although exhausted, the ripples carried on and swept over his feet. Canute turned to his attendants and said, 'Let the world know that the power of Kings is empty and worthless and cannot overcome He whose will the heavens and earth obey.'

Whether either of the above holds true, it is impossible to overlook the raw power of this 'Old Lady from Hull.' To watch its passing in daylight is awe-inspiring. The wave approaches the onlooker with menacing stealth, followed closely by its sibling waves known as 'whelps.' Osiers and willows on either bank bend to the will of the water as though supplicating before the presence of a passing deity. However, to encounter the Aegir at night, when the gloom and darkness, amplify the churn of the water, is an altogether different experience. The grinding roar of the water, magnified by the crepuscular murk, resembles the sound of a rapacious monster, impatient and insatiable. Those who make their living on the water speak of this turmoil as that of the river 'eating itself' or of fighting to save itself from being 'drowned from within.' They talk of the Aegir as though it is a living thing: 'Aegir'll be with us soon,' they say as someone might comment when looking forward to welcoming a returning friend or fearing the approach of an enemy.

In days gone by, in an attempt to appease the Aegir, it was the custom to throw a coin into the water, a practice which probably has its roots in Norse mythology when the offering of votives into water to appease the gods or bring good luck was widespread. There are those who still believe offering money to the Aegir will lessen its anger or at the very least absolve them from harm. 'Old timers,' speak of the river being greedy for life. Some even put a figure on the river's craving for life by stating it demanded and took up to seven lives a year. Farmers would willingly sacrifice their weakest lambs to the river in the belief that this might prove an adequate substitute for a human life. Though evidence reveals the number to be an overestimate there is little doubt that, across the centuries, the river has been responsible for a considerable loss of life. And when this happened, the sadness felt by others was often tempered by a period of relief; with a life taken, surely everyone was safe from the river's avarice for a while. During these times, parents would put aside their fears and allow their children to play on the slippery banks with impunity, safe in the knowledge that the river 'had taken its due!'

One of the earliest accounts of this dangerous river can be found in 'The Works of the Reverend John Wesley Vol. 2.' On Saturday 22 October 1743, he recounts arriving at the ferry crossing during a storm on his way from Epworth to Grimsby. Finding the boatmen reluctant to use their boats, Wesley and his companions waited an hour for the storm to pass. The storm lingered on however, and, not wanting to disappoint the congregation where he was due to preach, Wesley asked the men if they thought it was possible to get to the other shore. Their reply was non-committal, but they agreed if Wesley was prepared to 'venture his life they would venture theirs.' Wesley agreed and with five male companions, two females and three horses on board, the ferry boat set off. 'Many stood looking after us on the riverside, in the middle of which we were,' wrote Wesley, 'when in an instant, the side of the boat was under water, and the horses and men rolling one over another. We expected the boat to sink every moment, but I did not doubt being able to swim ashore. The boatmen were amazed as well as the rest, but they quickly recovered and rowed for their life. And soon after our horses leaping overboard lightened the boat, and we all came unhurt to land.' Once there, the boatmen asked Wesley why he did not rise from the bottom of the boat throughout the ordeal. After a quick inspection, he found that the lace of one of his shoes had snagged on an iron bar pinning him to the boat. Had the boat capsized, all agreed that he would have been unable to free himself and swim to shore. Keen to belittle the danger, Wesley saw it as the second time God had intervened to save his life; the first being from the fire at his rectory home. It turned out later, that on the same day and almost at the same time, his brother, Charles crossing the River Severn found his boat carried away in

The landing staithe and ferry point at the White Hart, Owston Ferry

a squall, narrowly avoiding being dashed on some nearby rocks. In his account, John exalted 'the same God, [who] when all human hope was past, delivered them as well as us.'

In the years before the Second World War thousands of 'tourists' headed to the river bank along the Axholme stretch to witness the Aegir; this 'Monster of the Trent.' Special excursions to see the Aegir ran by road from Lincoln, Doncaster, Worksop and Sheffield, the buses parking at accepted 'hotspots' to allow visitors to scramble up the banks and secure the best vantage point to view the spectacle. So great were the crowds in the village of Owston Ferry that special constables had to be drafted in to direct the traffic and control the arriving thrill seekers. Those who turned up to see an evening tide by car, parked on the top of the bank so the headlights, trained on the water, would give the onlookers a 'first-rate' view. Like others further downstream and those from decades past, they waited for the call of 'Ware Aegir!' to come rippling down the bank and signal the approaching wave; their excitement rising to a crescendo in a vocal parody to the advancing wave.

In September 1939, the curate of Owston Ferry 'rode' the Aegir with the local ferryman in a small rowing boat. Many regarded the vicar's 'excursion' as reckless and not a desirable undertaking for a man of the cloth, especially as Owston Ferry had the highest incidence of river tragedies. The pair endured a rough ride out but 'cruised' the wave with relative ease. The journey back to shore saw a very sick curate clinging limpet like to the structure of the boat. Thankfully both men arrived back at shore but so tight was the curate's hold on the thwarts of the boat that his hands had to be prised away by a couple of stout boatmen. Safe but soaked to the skin, the poor curate was so chastened by the experience that he vowed never to venture on the river again. The pair put their good fortune down to a tragedy that happened a few months earlier when Raymond Spencer of Brickyard Cottages, walking along the bank from West Butterwick to Owston Ferry, slipped and fell into the river. Although grappling operations began immediately, witnesses expressed surprise at how quickly Raymond's body disappeared beneath the surface of the water. Many believed the speed of Raymond's disappearance had assuaged the river's demands to the point that the curate and the ferryman's lives were never in danger.

In July 1876, one of the oldest reports of a river tragedy in a local newspaper recounted the death by drowning of the vivacious, eighteen-year-old daughter of Owston Ferry's, William Fletcher. At her point of entry, there were no signs of a struggle and no suspicion of suicide as all agreed she was a young lady with much to look forward to in life. Although several theories were advanced, what caused the calamity remains a mystery to this day.

Four years later, The Hull Packet* reported on a double drowning in the village. The first case concerned William Sykes, a fitter employed at Marshall's Foundry in Gainsborough. He and a plumber friend took a boat from a boatyard along the wharf and rowed down the Trent to the village. As they attempted to land at the jetty, William fell overboard disappearing beneath the water to rise only once. Rescuers recovered his body about an hour later. At the inquest, several witnesses stated that, in their opinion, even though the boat was not the cause of the tragedy, it was unfit to be afloat and requested the Coroner take 'such steps as may be necessary to have the said boat destroyed forthwith.' William left a widow and four children.

On the evening of the same day a boy, unnamed in the report, was riding with others in a horse-drawn cart down the high street. Something must have caused the horse to bolt, for without warning it set off at a gallop towards the Trent, dragging the wildly

---

Starting in 1787, the newspaper carried stories from Hull to Gainsborough. After four changes of title it adopted the The Hull Packet and East Riding Times in 1842. The paper was incorporated into The Hull Daily Mail in 1886.

careening cart along. All the occupants, except the young boy, managed to jump from the cart before the spooked horse plunged into the river. Thrashing violently, and encumbered by the harness of the vehicle, the horse's exertions pitched the boy into the river. Onlookers dashed to the spot and after concerted efforts managed to extricate the horse and recover the cart. They arrived too late, however, to rescue the poor boy whose body was swept away by the swirling current.

Three years later, and further downstream at Keadby, police constable Charles Hopkinson (22), described as a 'very promising young man,' was aboard a fishing smack some forty yards from shore. He was off duty so out of uniform when, on arriving close to shore, he saw a youth called Robert Bell with whom he needed to speak. He cast off from the vessel in a small cock boat but hadn't got far from the smack when the oar slipped from his grasp. Fearing he would be in an uncontrollable boat that carried him downstream, he attempted to leap back to the smack. His hands reached the vessel's side, but unable to secure a sufficiently sound grip he slipped into the water. Thrashing wildly, and unable to reach either craft he disappeared beneath the water before anyone on the smack could react. His body was not seen again.

Around the same time Mr. Andrews, proprietor of the ferry at Stockwith had a narrow escape from drowning. Along with a friend he had taken his large boat to Burringham to deliver a consignment of potatoes. On the way back, hoping to save valuable time, he arranged to have his boat towed by the steam packet. The experiment proved to be both dangerous and disastrous. The speed of the steamer, and the height of the wake created, caused Andrews' boat to fill rapidly with water. As the boat sank beneath them, the two men found themselves struggling in vain to keep the craft afloat. It was a hopeless task, and soon they were pitched into the churning water. The crew of the steamer rescued Andrews' friend, but in the pitch black water, they could not find Andrews. He had drifted away from the two boats while clinging to an oar. Eventually, as the crew swept the river with boat hooks in a last dispairing attempt to effect a rescue, one caught Andrews' trouser leg. Hauled on to the steamer by a relieved crew he was conveyed home in a state of severe shock. For many months he was left to rue the decision that cost him his boat, his livelihood and almost his life.

In early 1899, James Holmes, a seventy-year-old army pensioner sat in a public house in Owston Ferry enjoying a drink with his friends. As the evening drew to a close, he walked calmly out of the pub and headed for the river. With the utmost care, James took off his jacket, folded it neatly and placed it on the landing steps. As onlookers questioned his motives, he moved as close to the water as possible and, with barely a backward look, jumped into the river. He sank before aid could reach him. At the inquest, the coroner could find no evidence why James would do such a thing. Reluctantly he could bring in only one verdict - that James had committed suicide while being of unsound mind.

Further downstream, John Newton worked as the caretaker of sloops on Gunness Wharf. His job involved checking the rigging, the mooring and the security of a number of vessels. One night in April 1901 he was with Thomas Lowe and Walter Barber and, though they had been drinking, none were drunk. The men had just completed some final checks and were coming ashore. The night had darkened to the point that Lowe complained he could not see sufficiently well enough to climb the ladder to the top of the jetty and asked Newton to bring a lamp. Newton told him not to worry as 'it was not dark,' and they just had to follow him. He set off up the ladder but had only gone up a couple of steps when he 'seemed to disappear.' The two men following, heard a noise as if an object had struck one of the pilings and when they heard a splash they realised Newton had fallen into the Trent. Scrabbling around in the dark they attempted to latch on to some part of Newton's clothing to try and haul him out from between the pilings. They called out to him but received no response and assumed his head must have hit the side of the jetty, rendering him unconscious before he slipped into the water. As the night darkened the two men realised they had little hope of finding Newton's body, let alone rescuing him. The following morning, as the diffusing light of day spread across the wharf, John Newton's body could be seen jammed between the piles of the jetty, his head nodding sympathetically in concert with the flux of the river. At the inquest in the Ironstone Wharf Inn in Gunness, there was only one verdict the jury could return; the now familiar one of 'Accidentally Drowned.'

When Donovan Champion of Amcotts set off for a swim in the Trent with his two companions, they were looking forward to a gentle bathe in the river. After a period of horseplay, Donovan told his friends he was not content just to splash around and was going to swim across to the far bank. The announcement surprised his friends but they raised no alarm for they knew Donovan had both the strength and the ability to succeed in his venture. He had not gone far, however, when his friends realised he was in distress. One of them, a young boy called Clarke, made a valiant attempt to bring Donovan back to shore. Having reached him, he took a firm hold and keeping his head above water, headed for the bank. The pair were almost in reach of safety when Donovan just slipped from Clarke's grasp, disappeared beneath the waves, and did not resurface. His friends concluded that he must have had a seizure or fit of some kind as he was an excellent swimmer and had never before been in difficulties. Seven days later, and a mile or so from East Ferry, a group of river men examining some piles in the banking recovered Donovan's body in a severe state of putrefaction.

Despite these tragedies, beliefs persisted that crossing the river, especially by boat, brought the occupants luck. The ferrymen, in particular, always received a warm welcome wherever they went as many locals sought to profit from the river man's good fortune. At Christmas time especially the ferryman at Owston Ferry readily accepted the 'hospitality' of the Parish; free pints of beer being just one of the gifts on offer. Even on occasions when the ferryman stopped the boat during the crossing and lifted up his fishing rod to take advantage of a salmon run, no one criticised his actions. One notorious ferryman called Tom Mathers, came up with a novel way to boost his takings when demand for his services was low. Having agreed a fee of twopence, he would stop the boat in mid-stream and demand payment of sixpence instead, threatening to jump out of the boat and swim if the occupants didn't oblige. There are tales of him carrying out his threat and abandoning the boat to swim fully clothed to the far bank. We are not told what happened to the passengers!

One of the greatest tragedies to occur on the river, however, happened on a fine, temperate, August Bank Holiday Monday in 1917. The residents of Owston Ferry eager to put aside the travails of a war entering its fourth year, turned out in huge numbers to see the passing of the Aegir. The predictions were, that this was going to be memorable Aegir and as events unfolded so it proved. From the surrounding villages, visitors arrived on horseback and by pony and trap, while the more athletic restored to pedal power. Others, from as far afield as Sheffield, Leeds and Nottingham, arrived chatting and giggling on open-topped charabancs and omnibuses, specially commissioned for the day. There was a carnival atmosphere all around with shopkeepers and stallholders looking forward to a good return from the day's trading. Several local boatmen had loosened the ropes that moored their boats, and some even rowed them to the middle of the river to anchor them there. Much better if the boat could float 'freely' than run the risk of it smashing against the jetty in the viscious churn of the Aegir.

At the White Hart jetty, Alf Torn, the thirty-year-old ferryman made some last minute adjustments to his boat. Strong in the arm and shoulder, Alf was an excellent swimmer and knew the river's moods like no other. Having crossed and re-crossed its turbulent swirls and eddies up to a dozen times a day, he had little to fear from its most treacherous of currents. He knew the Aegir well and had negotiated it on many occasions, taking thrill-seeking passengers into mid-stream to ride the approaching wave. To an experienced ferryman, it was a risk worth taking, so much so that he was never short of willing passengers. It was a day he'd looked forward to; a public holiday with plenty of eager 'tourists,' a balmy evening with the light 'holding just long enough' and a high tide with the potential to give sufficient lift to his boat, providing the occupants with a memorable experience. As he locked in his oars, he looked towards the landing and smiled. It was a smile of reassurance, as much for himself as for the eleven passengers lined up and waiting

A cyclist waits to cross the river as the ferryman manoeuvres into position.

to board. In the main, the line consisted of well-dressed young ladies, but Alf's eyes fixed on one of only two men – his brother, Robert. Alf gave him a barely discernible nod of the head and received a similar response from Robert. It was time to go!

With Robert helping on the jetty and Alf holding out a steadying hand, the boat began to fill. Last to board, Robert took up his position on the stern thwart and leaning back released the craft from its moorings. As Alf struck out into the fast flowing water, from nowhere the body of a young girl landed in an inelegant heap amongst those settling down for the voyage. Too late to turn round for fear of not being in the right position in mid-stream, Alf asked everyone one to shuffle up and make room for the new arrival. A few hefty strokes later, they were on their way when a guttural cry rang out from shore: 'Thas gotten thoteen in't bowat Alf, nay good'll come on it!' It drew a hush from the crowd, sufficiently quiet enough for those of an experienced ear to pick up the near-distant roar of the approaching wave. The sound, described by some as the river 'turning against itself,' and others as though it was 'devouring itself from within,' saw many turn their gaze north eager for their first sight of 'the Old Lady.'

Knowing that turning around would risk placing his boat broadside on to the Aegir, Alf began to angle his boat end on to the approaching wave. He was just completing this manoeuvre when the wave hit. Initially, all seemed well as the boat lifted on the swell but, as it dipped, the successive waves set the boat rocking. Although Alf tried to reassure the passengers that the boat could ride this out, some in their panic began to stand up. This increased the undulations and destabilised the boat further. Spectators on the bank watched as the horror began to unfold. As though in slow motion the boat pitched sideways spilling most of the occupants into the surging tide. Cries from those on the riverbank rang out, matching the screams from the water.

Looking north toward the Crooked Billet, Owston Ferry - circa 1900

Onlookers, who a few minutes earlier had been waving to their friends in the ill-fated craft, rushed to launch boats. Some of the stronger swimmers pitched into the water fully clothed to try to help with the rescue. In this way, they managed to save eleven of the fourteen occupants. In one rescue, a woman had to thank her long hair which floated on the surface of the water as she struggled beneath the waves. Reaching out and grabbing hold of her flowing tresses, her rescuer hauled the distressed woman to the surface before dragging her into the safety of a rescue boat. In a desperate attempt to save themselves, two ladies, Margaret Brunton, a forty-year-old housekeeper and Alice Withers (18), both employed at the White Hart, wrapped their arms around Alf Torn's neck. Strong swimmer though he was, their weight overcame his ability to stay afloat until help arrived and all three sank below the waves. Those saved included Mrs. Dearden and Mr. Farewell Fox from Attercliffe; George Guest (4) and Marjorie Guest (14) son and daughter of the proprietor of the White Hart; Miss Brunton, sister of the one of those drowned; Miss Cissie Gleadhill, daughter-in-law of the ferrymen; Mr. Robert Torn, the ferryman's brother; Misses Frances Forster and Doris Barker, maids at Hemdyke House and Miss Bicky Holah of Crowle.

The ferryman's cottage at Owston Ferry.

At the inquest, the coroner commented on the decision to allow 12 people into the boat and confirmed it was the contributing factor to it capsizing. He did not regard the negotiation of such a tidal wave as being risky for an experienced ferryman, but the number of inexperienced boaters and incautious holidaymakers out to experience a thrill had the effect of significantly raising the level of danger. Some witness reports suggest the three bodies were found together, with the two ladies still clinging to Alf's body but this was little more than speculative embellishment. Sometime later, Alf's 'unaccompanied' body was recovered three-quarters of a mile down river. He left a widow and seven children. The body of Margaret Brunton turned up at West Stockwith a day and a half later; there is no record of anyone recovering Alice's body.

As for the rescued – despite a terrible experience most of them recovered quickly, but several vowed never to use the ferry again. The accident left a profound sadness throughout the district. In particular, it was a chastening experience for the village and filled many who used the ferry boat regularly with foreboding (particularly for parents from East Ferry whose children crossed the river twice daily when attending school in Owston Ferry).

The playing field memorial to the three boys.

As the century unfolded, deaths by drowning continued sporadically, but by the 1980s it seemed the terrors of the Trent had become a thing of the past. All this changed in 1987 when, almost seventy years to the day following the ferry boat disaster, the river claimed three more victims. The circumstances and details of the event remain raw, and it would be insensitive to delve too deeply into the specifics here. Of the four boys driving a car along the river bank, only one managed to escape when it plunged into the water.

For many who lived along its course, the river was the chief source of water for washing and, for a small number, drinking. Before the arrival of piped water in the mid-twentieth century, each house had to be self-sufficient in its supply of water. One source was spring water, and the sinking of a well was usually the first operation undertaken before laying the foundations of a house. This water was, in theory at least, relatively pure and safe to drink, especially when passed through a ceramic charcoal filter. It had a hardness, however, that did not suit laundering as it caused soap to 'curdle.' For doing the weekly wash and other scullery tasks, most people used rainwater. The nearness of a large body of water such as the river, however, saw some turn to the Trent to 'draw' their water. When the rural council instructed everyone living along its banks to stop taking water from the river for drinking for fear of typhus and suggested they install tanks to collect rainwater, several residents objected.

One protester was Edward Jones of Gunthorpe who wrote a stinging response to the council in which he stated; 'I live by myself on a property left by my father, and have one of the finest freshwater rivers in England flowing past my house. I have lived by the river for 50 years, and my father before me, and have never used any other for drinking purposes. The river water is far better than rainwater, taking all reasons together. Where tanks have been supplied to people in the villages, they still continue to use Trent water for drinking, as the taste suits them better than rainwater. I do not know why the authority are (sic) compelling owners to go to this unnecessary expense, unless it is that they can continue to pour the filthy sewage of the town [Gainsborough] into the river, to the danger of the people on the riverside.' In reply, the council stated they had done all they could and insisted that new houses had a certificate saying they would be supplied with 'wholesome' water. They also advised people to stop diverting their sewage into the river but recognised until this happened 'cases of typhoid would occur on a regular basis.'

CHAPTER TWO

Customs

MYTH AND MAYHEM

By far the best known Axholme tradition, and one of the oldest traditional events in England, is that of Haxey Hood. There can be few Islonians who do not recognise the terms, 'Lord,' 'Fool' and 'Boggin' or the famous refrain that begins 'Hoose agen hoose, toon agen toon.'

The event takes place on 6 January, the Twelfth Day of Christmas, seen by some as linking it to the onset of Epiphany, a period of insight and inspiration in the Christian calendar. The event draws on fifteenth-century customs held each Plough Monday when ploughmen traditionally blackened their faces to mark the end of the Christmas period. To help raise money they would drag a decorated plough around the larger houses in their village. Often accompanied by someone dressed outlandishly and acting the Fool, they would call out 'Penny for the ploughboys!' The character of the Fool also appears in plays enacted on Plough Monday, a universal theme being resurrection. His presence, with a blackened face, is said to evoke the idea of rebirth. At some point in the late Middle Ages, the traditions of the Hood may have also drawn in elements from Shrove Tuesday football-like games of the sort still played at Ashborne in Derbyshire and Workington in Cumbria.

Other theories link the event to the Celtic festival of mid-winter where animal sacrifices (and in some instances human) feasting and gift giving were common elements of the season. The premise for this argument is that of a game where scrimmages

Lady Mowbray loses her hood - from the Haxey Kneeler Tapestry

took place for the head of a bullock (the most prized part of the animal). Being a 'beast of the plough,' the expectation was that such a sacrifice would bring better crops during the coming year. Those who support this argument point to the Old English word for hide being 'hude,' cementing further the links to the sacrifice of a bullock. This argument also draws on the ritual of purification by smoke; the smoking of the Fool being a key ingredient of the event in Haxey. Some historians associate the game with the Celtic rite of sun worship maintaining the course of the hood through the air represents the passage of the sun through the upper heavens; the struggle to gain possession of it bestowing favourable weather upon its keepers. In support of this theory they claim the twelve attendant boggins each represent a sign of the Zodiac.

The most commonly held belief, however, links the custom to the Mowbray family, Lords of the Manor of Axholme from a time just after the Conquest to the late fifteenth century. The tale of Lady Mowbray losing her hood while riding through the Isle fields and being amused as plough hands fought over it in their enthusiasm to return it, has become a story embedded in Axholme

As the smoke swirls around, the Fool delivers his speech

folklore. Lord and Lady Mowbray did exist; John de Mowbray being the most likely candidate for the spouse of the lady who lost her hood. It was this John, whose deed some 650 years ago, granted land to the commoners; a radical decision at the time, so perhaps this gave the rustics another reason to celebrate.

One of the earliest accounts of the 'game' appears in William Peck's 'Topographical Account of the Isle of Axholme' published in 1815. It is he who connects the Haxey custom with the 'ordinary Twelfth-tide mummers or plough-jags' of the county. Peck narrative differs slightly from the game as it is played today as he writes that 'a roll of canvas tightly corded together, weighing from four to six pounds, was taken to an open field and contended for by the rustics, who assemble together to the number of many hundreds; an individual appointed casts it from him, and the first person that can convey it into the cellar of any public-house receives a reward of one shilling, paid by the plough-bullocks or hoggins. A new hood being furnished when the others are carried off, the contest usually continues till dark. The next day the plough-bullocks or hoggins go round the town to receive alms at each house, where they cry "Largus." They are habited similar to the Morris Dancers, are yoked to and drag a small plough. They have their farmer and a fool, called

Billy Buck, dressed like a harlequin, with whom the boys make sport. The day concludes with the plough-bullocks running with the plough round the cross in the marketplace, and the man that can throw the others down and convey their plough into the cellar of a public-house receives one shilling for his agility.'

In his 'History and Topography of the Isle of Axholme' published twenty-four years later, Reverend William Stonehouse records the festival as 'a sport or game peculiar to the place.' He goes on: 'The hood is a piece of sacking rolled tightly up and well corded which weighs about six pounds. This is taken into an open field on the north side of the church about two o'clock in the afternoon, to be contended for by the youths assembled for that purpose. When the hood is about to be thrown up, the plough-bullocks, or boggins, as they are called, dressed in scarlet jackets, are placed amongst the crowd at certain distances. Their persons are sacred, and if amidst the general row the hood falls into the hands of one of them the sport begins again. The object of the person who seizes the hood is to carry off the prize to some public-house in the town, where he is rewarded with such liquor as he chooses to call for. This pastime is said to have been instituted by the Mowbrays.'

Newspaper reports in the Stamford Mercury from the 1840s take up the story in greater detail. They speak of 'having an old sack, or something of the sort wrapped up and carried in procession through the village by a person dressed in the true Tom Fool style, attended by his twelve satellites, ydept Boggans, equipped in jerkins of red and ribbons.' When the procession reaches an open space near the church 'the leader harangues the mobility assembled, who by this time often amount to 2000 to 3000, reciting to them the laws and regulations of the sport.' Later, 'the commander (alias the Fool), surrounded by his twelve good men and true at a distance of 100 yards or so, throws up the hood (old bag), which is the signal for commencing a general strife.'

When the paper's correspondents move from relaying the events of the day to commenting on the custom, however, they reveal their aversion to the day's event. One goes on to say 'this silly game originated in the remote ages of ignorance and barbarism. In their coarse amusement, the participators expose themselves to unnumbered kicks and bruises, shins are broken, eyes blackened, and noses made to spout streams of blood which are visible on the land for weeks after. When the game is finished, the village to which the ball (sic) has been taken presents a scene of riotous intemperance which baffles all description. It is surprising that the authorities should permit such proceedings.'

Other newspaper reports from this period are equally disparaging. One refers to the participants 'taste for enjoyment rising no higher than a kick about in the dirt for several hours [after] a piece of old sacking tied up something after the way in which a gentleman wraps up his top coat before it is strapped to the saddle.' He goes on to speak of 'the participants in this recreation [exposing] themselves to innumerable kicks and bruises with perchance a broken bone or two.' Another report entitled 'Ancient Sports on the Trentside – Haxey,' speaks of one of the hoods being 'taken to Craiselound (sic), and the other triumphantly to Wroot, by three brothers.' Following the day's action 'the night was spent in drinking and carousing, and other unmanly proceedings.' It seems Plough Monday, generally the first Monday after 6 January which was a merry day across the country 'in times of yore,' passed off quietly in Axholme as locals recovered from the effects of wounding or drink!

A few years later correspondents from the Stamford Mercury write of 'the hood being basted with ale,' while the participants 'get excessively drunk, and bacchanalian orgies are kept up for a week and upwards, the never-failing consequences being sundry broken limbs [and] black eyes, for it is an established maxim that all old grudges and back reckonings are to be cleared up. All [of] which can be done with impunity. The farmers are considerable sufferers by having their new-sown wheat trodden up, their fences broken down and their turnips pulled up in the most shameful manner, these serving as convenient missiles for the belligerent parties. And, to perpetuate this foolish, wicked, and utterly useless custom, the inhabitants almost to an individual provide for and invite their friends; even farmers and respectable householders encourage it by giving money or corn to the Boggans (sic) who go from house to house for the purpose of begging and wind up the whole by tying up the master of ceremonies in a tree, and making a fire of wet straw under it to smoke him black – thus making his outward appearance approach a little nearer the colour of his benighted intellect.'

Other correspondents, however, took a different viewpoint. One wrote of the village holding the occasion in such esteem that it presented 'a most animated appearance, both from the assembling of local friends, and others from a considerable distance.' The article referred to 'a kind of mock introduction, fraught like most other rural sports with a whimsical peculiarity,' where the contending parties commence the game 'with the throwing of the hood, each striving to get it to their respective parish with a spirit of manliness which carries back the mind to those good old games of feudalism [before] physical skill and energy were debased by luxurious refinement.' The correspondent who wrote this must have felt a close affinity with the event for he concludes: 'To those who wonder why the authorities should permit such proceedings, I can only say, with the usual courtesy that since the scene is appalling to their tender feelings, it would be better to abstain in future from visiting the terrible field of action.'

Today, the rules, reinforced by the Fool's speech, state that the hood should be 'swayed,' i.e. pushed from the field towards a local hostelry. Running with the hood is not allowed. Once touched by the sway, trespass becomes 'no law' and the participants have the freedom to access all areas. Over the years, however, not everyone has played the game by the rules. During the Second World War, a troop of soldiers billeted locally managed to smuggle the hood to the Red Lion in Owston Ferry by concealing it down the trouser leg of one of the servicemen and driving off in a jeep! Thirty-four years later Reg Rockliffe and David Palmer secretly 'lifted' the hood and calmly walked with it to the Kings Arms. In the darkness, when one of the sways broke up, the pair found themselves alone and in possession of the Hood. While those in the recovering sway scrabbled around to find it, the two young men casually strolled off the field. No one challenged them, so they kept going until handing the Hood over to Stan Jarvis, landlord of the King's Arms. The incident generated much criticism from the purists who insisted that it was the sway that must deliver the Hood to the landlord. In a letter in the Epworth Bells, one contributor wrote, 'the two men should be ashamed of themselves, especially as they are local men and know the rules. The landlord had no right to accept a Hood that had not been 'swayed' and should have given it back to the Lord or boggins for the game to be restarted.' One of the longest sways on record was that of 1948 when, after hours of struggle over fields, through ditches and along dykes, the hood, thrown up by Captain Crookshank, the local Member of Parliament, found its way to the Great Northern Hotel at Park Drain. The 'shortest' Hood happened in 2015 when it reached the Loco public house in one hour thirty-five minutes.

Over the years the popularity of 'The Hood' has fluctuated; in the late nineteenth century, some local moralist took delight in writing that this 'coarse amusement' had all but lost its following. A revival took place in the 1920s possibly as a means of reasserting community life after the destruction wrought by the Great War. Today, despite increased regulations to ensure the safety of participants and onlookers, and the closure of supporting public houses, this renaissance continues.

Another Haxey custom on Hood Day but carried out at the school, was that of 'locking in' the headteacher. This action supposedly gave pupils the chance to leave school and watch the events on Hood Field. Generally the headteacher endured this in good spirits but, unfortunately, some pupils took to abusing the ritual, inflicting it on the head at other times of the year. In February 1874, eighteen girls reversed this custom and locked the mistress out of school at one o'clock. Having secured the door, they made sure the mistress couldn't use her key by sealing the entrance with wedges. Finally gaining access at 1.30 p.m. the mistress spared none when reprimanding the culprits. Almost a year to the day later, the boys locked the head out of the school at lunchtime. Their punishment is not on record, but that of Ernest Torr is. In 1895, having locked the head out of the school and hidden the key, he received 'six cuts of the cane' when caught.

Perhaps the most perverse school custom was a long established convention in Owston Ferry. A child caught misbehaving would be dispatched to the school garden with the headmaster's penknife with instructions to cut a branch from the willow tree in the corner of the yard. Upon their return, the master used this stick to administer the requisite punishment!

A little-known fact is that right up to the beginning of the twentieth century both Epworth and Belton held 'Hood Days.' First recorded in the 1815 edition of Peck's account, the Epworth Hood had been kept in the King's Head Hotel since 1880 and only released for the game on the payment of 15 shillings. In 1887 the Epworth Bells reported 'a great many inhabitants turn[ed] out, despite the bad weather' to take part in this 'ancient custom.' The Epworth Hood was similar to the one at Haxey but with some distinct variations. Played on the fields behind St. Andrew's

Church, the competing teams did not push the Hood away from the field to a local hostelry, but to 'certain goals.' These posts when struck three times saw the hood declared 'free' for the game to start again. Locals called this action 'Wyking the Hood.' The game, itself, was usually played on the same day (6 January) as the one at Haxey, though there is some evidence that it could take place on other days by request. The Hood game at Belton took place over the open fields with goals at Churchtown and Westgate. Not surprisingly, the people of Haxey looked upon these 'games' as mere imitations of the 'real thing.'

Further evidence from Peck shows Morris Dancing in Epworth was a fixture at Church fetes and May Day celebrations by the mid-eighteenth century. Unable to afford rich costumes the agricultural labourers resorted to ordinary clothing decorated with ribbons and flowers. The dances, typical of most Morris celebrations, took many forms from processional promenades to group jigs and used a variety of props such as handkerchiefs, wooden shaft handles and swords. The custom flourished for a while before dying out in the early 1800s.

One custom that also prevailed in Epworth, and possibly other

---

EPWORTH HOOD.

THE HOOD will be thrown up in the Church Field, at TWO o'clock, on THURSDAY Afternoon, January 7th, 1886; and is to be given up at the Temperance Hall, where the PRIZES will be given in tickets representing value in kind—not money.

A Committee has been formed, of which Mr. T. BROOKS, Belton-road, is the Treasurer.

The next Meeting of the Committee will be on Tuesday evening next, Jan. 5th, at the Temperance Hall, at 7.30.

Extracted from The Epworth Bells

Isle communities for a while, was that of 'Riding the Stange.' This was 'punishment by public ridicule' and acted out on a husband suspected of beating his wife. The 'event' began around eight o'clock in the evening when young men from the town (and perhaps a few children), assembled near the door of the suspected offender. The crowd began the ridicule by beating kettles and pans; blowing on cow's horns and whistles, and shouting and yelling. The 'rider,' mounted across a ladder and carried on men's shoulders would then begin reciting the rhyme:

With a ran, dan, dan, at the sign of the old tin can,
For neither your case, nor my case do I ride the stange.
For Johnny* has been beating his wife *(*insert name of offender)*
He beat her, he bang'd her, he bang'd her indeed.
He bang'd her, poor creature, before she stood need.

This ritual would be repeated on three successive nights, after which the culprit was left to think over the manner he treated his wife. If little or nothing changed, then the 'stange' would appear again.

Crowle too had a marital custom called 'Falling Out.' If a couple who had 'kept company' for some time happened to quarrel, and afterwards the man married another woman (or the woman married a man), on the eve of the wedding, the neighbours would tie a cabbage to the door of the jilted party. The message was plain, cabbages widely regarded as the vegetable of the poor, were insignificant as was the soon to be married ex-partner.

And finally, while on the subject of Isle marriages, by far the most bizarre wedding to occur in Axholme took place on 26 November 1811 when, after a courtship of one night, seventy-year-old Robert Berry, a beehive manufacturer from Beltoft married fifteen-year-old Miss Jane Easton, a flax dresser from Ealand!

CHAPTER THREE

Danger on the Highway

MISADVENTURE

We tend to associate road safety with the motoring age. It is an indisputable fact, however, that there were more deaths on the roads of Axholme before the advent of the motor car than there have been since. Up to the early twentieth-century, well-drained, crushed stone tarmacadam roads were a rarity for residents and travellers of the Isle. Some of the roads in the towns and villages had reasonable surfaces with cobbled areas and granite setts, but just about every other road was left unsurfaced. On these routes, one method was merely to spread a layer of broken rock and gravel on the cleared foundation of earth. Another was to leave them to become routes of compacted soil. Here, the narrow treads of the farmers' wagons cut ruts into the land, and the hooves of animals disturbed the ground further. Where the road became rutted, everyone took a route that seemed the best at the time. After rain, this created a wide disturbed mess that in many cases proved to be impassable.

It would, however, be wrong to lay the blame for accidents purely on road conditions. What holds true today regarding driver error can be applied to horse-driven vehicles on the Isle at least up to the middle of the twentieth century and in some isolated cases, beyond. Much as now, such accidents fell into four categories. Careless driving often resulted in carriages turning corners too fast, driving up banks, into ditches, or crashing into other vehicles or obstacles. Furious driving, thankfully, not a frequent cause of accidents even though there were no penalties for it. A third cause was negligence. There was no driving test to determine a person's competence when in charge of a horse and vehicle, so ignorance and inexperience were no barriers to road usage. Finally, and an all too common sight, was driving under the influence of alcohol. Trap and wagon drivers, however, did have one extra problem to contend with - the unpredictable behaviour of the horse! Those holding the reins often had to contend with a horse (or horses) bolting, shying, rearing, jibbing, falling or kicking. From fast-moving traps to heavy and cumbersome wagons, those in control often picked the best route forward and hoped for the best. It was not always the route the horse sought to follow! Although shared spaces, many of the 'roads' on the Isle were too narrow to accommodate pedestrians and horse driven-vehicles. The accepted 'rule' left the onus on those travelling by foot to step from the pathway to allow the right of way to a horse rider or horse-driven carriage. It was a practical and sensible rule born out of rank and superiority, but when observed correctly it worked well.

On a bright Saturday in January 1860, passengers on the market coach that ran from the Isle to Doncaster market asked the driver to slow down so they could take in the view across the racecourse. He had just acceded to their request when the spokes on one of the wheels broke, causing the coach to lurch to the side of the road. Before the driver could rein in the horses further, the coach pitched on its side 'with great violence.' Those riding inside the coach escaped serious injury, though several received cuts and bruises that required attention later. However, the two gentlemen riding on the top of the coach fared much worse. Pitched to the ground, Mr. Adams, a gentleman of some note, journeying to Sheffield on business, suffered severe head injuries and Mr. Sergeant of Blaxton Grange sustained a dislocated shoulder. Thankfully all recovered from their ordeal, but the consensus was that, had the coach been travelling at its usual speed and not slowing, fatalities would have resulted.

On 11 February of the same year, three people returning home at night from Doncaster market in a wagon driven by Thomas Binks suffered the ultimate fate. As he drove along a snow-covered Sanderson Bank to the west of Westwoodside, somehow Thomas lost control of the horses on a road flanked to this day by deep ditches. Riding with Thomas in the cart was his wife Sarah, his brother-in-law Thomas Wagstaff, John Whitehead, and a gentleman called Mr. Gleadall. They were heading for Bullhassocks, where the Binks family managed a farm of four hundred acres. Reports from the time suggest that the group were returning home in a rather 'merry' state, having called at The Bank End Inn (The Horse and Stag), on the Yorkshire/Nottinghamshire border, after leaving the crossroads at Blaxton.* Thomas Binks and Gleadall survived the crash, but the other three died as the cart tumbled into the ditch on the north side of the road. Wagstaff and Webster drowned in the ditch after being pinned there by the overturning cart; Sarah died when she was struck and crushed by a loose beer barrel. To the observant traveller, a memorial stone, placed by the side of the carriageway just after the crossroads at Park Drain, can still be seen marking the location where the accident happened. The family must have been held in high esteem as the funding for the stone came from local donations. In addition to naming the individuals who died, the epitaph concludes: 'Who can tell what day can bring forth. In the midst of life we are in death. Be ye also ready.'

In the latter years of the nineteenth-century, a rash of trap and cart accidents occurred on the Isle, several resulting in fatalities. When twenty-seven-year-old William Henry Jackson of Amcotts set off with Mr. Belton's cart, there seemed little cause for concern. William was a competent horseman and an experienced cart driver,

---

* *This later became the Bank End Park Hotel. There is now later housing along Sanderson Bank Lane and only part of the disused Hotel remains.*

The memorial stone erected by public subscription along Sanderson Bank.

but this experience counted for little when, without warning, the horses 'took off.' Struggling to rein them in, William lost all control when the reins broke away. The horses dragged the wagon 'some distance' before it overturned into a drain, pinning William underneath. Witnesses rushed to his aid and succeeded in pulling him out, but it was clear he had sustained a severe injury to the head. Attending the scene, Dr. Bernhardt pronounced 'severe concussion of the brain' and supervised his removal home. According to reports in the newspaper, William 'lingered' for almost a week before he died.

On the afternoon of 2 September 1884, James Markham, a cottager of Kelfield, was driving his cart close to home. In the back sat his wife and his sister. Suddenly, in what some believed was the horse's desire to get home quickly, the animal bolted forward. James, controlling the horse with only a single line, put his feet on the shaft in an attempt to jump from the cart to try to control the horse from the ground. As he did so his feet slipped and he fell backwards. His body took the full force of the cart as the wheels of the vehicle passed over him breaking his thigh and causing massive internal injuries. The unattended horse clattered on with the two women clinging to the sides of the cart in the hope they could remain attached. However, as the horse attempted to turn through a gateway into a cornfield, the front of the vehicle caught a gatepost, and the sudden jolt pitched the occupants to the ground. Luckily both suffered only minor injuries, and they were soon on their feet heading back to where James lay. As they drew near both realised they were looking at a fatality. Men at work in a nearby field heard their cries for help and rushed to the scene. They, too, were quick to realise there was little practical help they could give. While one went off to fetch a doctor, others went in search of the runaway horse. They found it close to the farm lying on its back exhausted, shackled by the shafts of the upturned cart. When the doctor arrived he confirmed what all knew – James had died from massive internal bleeding.

Perhaps the saddest of all reports concerning 'conveyance' related deaths were the ones involving young children. One such, in October 1869, saw Mr. Lee, a baker from Crowle, loading his cart before his delivery round with the shafts propped upwards. When he went into his shop to get more loaves he left his three and a half-year-old son, Albert, playing nearby. Albert no doubt saw the cart as an attractive plaything and he began swinging on the back. It was the section of the cart that was most heavily ladened and Albert's extra weight caused it to tip down, crushing the poor boy beneath. When his father returned, he quickly dragged Albert's limp body out from beneath the cart. It was to no avail, however, as half an hour later the little boy died in his father's arms!

Five years later, also in Crowle, fifteen-year-old Edward Harrison of Leam House Farm was at work helping men plough with four pairs of horses. At half past five work stopped and the men released the horses from their plough shafts. From his first day at work, Edward had an affinity with the farm horses and the ploughmen recognised the ease with which he handled each one.

They were happy to hand over their care to Edward, confident in his ability to attend to the needs of each horse. For his part, Edward did not see them as beasts of burden - they were friends to be nurtured and embraced. After a few comforting words, Edward swung himself on to the back of one of a pair, perhaps intending to ride it back to the farm. Almost immediately and without warning, the horse and its ploughing partner bolted and as they pitched 'round and round' Edward fell off catching his legs in the tangle of traces. As the horses galloped away, his body was jerked along the ground for thirty yards as one might see a rag doll being yanked by an irresponsible child. Unable to free himself Edward was dragged beneath the iron-clad hooves. Spared any further suffering when the horses came to rest Edward tried to communicate with the ploughmen who rushed to his aid but the severity of his injuries rendered him incapable of speech. In this state of distress, Edward clung on to life for half an hour before passing away.

In the early summer of 1897, Thomas Brown was driving his horse and dray up the street in Owston Ferry. A kindly soul, Thomas always attracted a large crowd of children and would often allow them to climb onto his dray for a ride. From here they would chat and sing and shout out to others to come and join them. On this day, Tuesday 25 May, five-year-old Solomon Qualter heard the cries from those on board and ran out to join them. He attempted to get onto the dray as it moved past him but slipped and fell beneath the back wheel. The whole weight of the wagon passed over his little body. Onlookers rushed to the boy's aid and carried him to the doctor's. The surgeon's frantic efforts to revive the poor boy proved futile; Solomon's injuries were too extensive, and he died some minutes later. The accident caused a rethink over the lackadaisical and negligent way some carters and draymen approached their tasks. Many people described how they often drove 'extravagantly, fiercely or furiously.' It was not the case with

Thomas who was not blamed for the death of poor little Solomon, but his actions on that day would haunt him for the rest of his life.

Finally in this section comes the report of the shocking death of twelve-year-old Hannah Clark, daughter of William Clark, a farm labourer from Belton. Hannah and two friends were playing in an unattended cart on fields in Samuel Closes. The horse in the shafts suddenly took fright and headed for the field gateway. The cart struck a gatepost and overturned, crushing Hannah beneath. Death was instantaneous. Of the other two girls, one suffered a broken leg while the other escaped unhurt. As with so many of the above cases, the coroner returned a verdict of 'Accidental Death.'

There was a fixed fine of ten shillings for being drunk in charge of a horse and trap, a fee many magistrates considered too lenient. One of those was Alderman Blaydes of Epworth, a strict adherent of the Temperance Movement. He often sought ways to increase the financial punishment for drunken behaviour and when Fred Tillotson Turner of Crowle was called to court at Epworth police station on 15 July 1886, after being found drunk while in charge of a horse and trap, he accepted he would have to pay the ten shilling fine. He expected Alderman Blaydes to fine him the requisite ten shillings but imagine his astonishment when the doughty Alderman ordered him to pay court costs amounting to thirty-six shillings!

Not all bolting horses led to tragedy, however, and some scenes involving wild horses and owners desperate catch up with them, must have resembled episodes from the 'Keystone Cops.' One can only imagine the sight as owners chased after their runaway beast and people in the street stepped forward waving their arms in a frantic attempt to grab hold of the horse's bridle as it cantered past. In one incident, the horse belonging to John Hill of Epworth slipped its harness while he was in Burnham making deliveries. The startled animal shot off up the hill towards Epworth and cantered down Burnham Road to the High Street. Here it turned left and headed west for over a mile with the trap bouncing and swerving behind. Both came to a rest in Ellers' Lane, two miles from their starting point. There were several narrow escapes along the way but neither horse, human nor trap suffered lasting damage.

While playing in the road close to their home in April 1871, Alfred Pyatt and Alice Maw from Crowle, aged seven and five respectively, were bitten by a dog. When both slipped into a coma, the doctor suspected the dog might have had rabies. Despite his efforts, the children developed hydrophobia and died from 'breathing failure.' Where the animal came from, or to whom it belonged, could not be established but there were warnings to the public to be watchful for stray and even pet dogs. Local constables were empowered to destroy all animals running free, an edict that caused many individuals to question such sweeping powers.

Before moving from accidents on four legs to those on four wheels let us pause to examine some unfortunate accidents that happened on two or in the following example, three wheels. Patrick Daley (66) a hawker in the area and originally from Dublin was found badly injured beneath an old tricycle he had bought the day before in Wroot. A police constable who examined the machine declared it to be 'a worn out affair' with brakes that were 'altogether unworkable.' It seems Patrick was cycling from Haxey to Burnham when he lost control of the tricycle on the hill just beyond the windmill. Unable to brake, he took the corner at too fast a speed and headed off the road into the fields of Kimber Farm. Initially thought to have suffered minor cuts and bruises, and having no family to care for him, the police took Patrick to the workhouse infirmary at Gainsborough. His injuries must have been far worse than at first thought because two weeks later Patrick died. At the inquest, the jury returned the customary verdict of 'Accidental Death,' and ordered the police to 'knock the tricycle to pieces before anyone else came to harm.'

By far the saddest accident of the many that happened on

Burnham Hill was one in 1934 involving Arthur Brown (66) and Olive Garnett (14) who was killed outright. Witnesses stated that Olive, cycling down the hill at a reasonable pace, was on the proper side of the road. Brown driving up the hill following a van accelerated to enable his car to move smoothly up the steepest part of the gradient. In his statement to the police, he said that as he reached the crown of the bend 'all of a sudden a cyclist appeared from behind the van and headed towards him.' As he swerved to the near side, he felt a collision just before the car mounted the kerb and turned over, coming to rest thirty-three yards from the point of impact. His impression was that the cyclist must have swerved towards him. Horace Kitching, who saw the van and car before the accident said he formed the opinion that the vehicles were racing. After examining Olive's bike, the police found it had no front brake and an inefficient back one. At his trial, Brown pleaded not guilty to murder and the jury returned the same verdict. It was not the end of the story, however, as Olive's family placed a white cross at the crash site, ostensibly as a memorial to their daughter but also to create a painful reminder to all drivers of the dangerous nature of the hill. The cross (minus the top part in later years) remained in place until the council removed it to widen the road at the crown of the bend,

One of the most serious accidents, and one in which fate played a large part, occurred in Epworth in December 1944. The three Mellers brothers were outside the West End council house of the eldest, Frederick. It was Frederick's birthday, and he and his brothers, Albert and William, were enjoying reminiscing about incidents from his early youth. Approaching them from Sandtoft was a Hillman 10 driven by Jacob Clark of Rectory Street. Having driven from Newland to deliver a potato spinner to a farm in Sandtoft, John was on his way back with an empty trailer. Freed from its counterweight the trailer was less stable and along the bumpy road from the River Torne it had been bouncing up and down and from side-to-side. Aware of this, Clark had slowed down to a respectable speed of 25 miles an hour. As the car entered the town and approached the row of council houses, there was a loud noise and the trailer broke loose. It veered to the off side of the road and headed in the direction of the three men. They had no time to react as the trailer mounted the kerb, skidded across the grass verge and ploughed into them, flinging one yards through the air and dragging the other two underneath as it careered on before coming to rest some yards away. Clark stopped immediately and rushed from the car to assist the badly injured men. Along with Arthur Colley, a passenger in a following car, he helped carry one of them into the house. The driver of that car, Ernest Jackson from Owston Ferry, then drove off to fetch a doctor. It was Dr. Macregor who arrived and pronounced Frederick dead at the scene from a fracture to the base of the neck. He arranged for Albert and William to be taken to the War Memorial Hospital in Scunthorpe. Later that night Albert died in hospital from 'extensive injuries.'

At the inquest, the jury heard that Clark had driven lorries and tractors, but it was only the second time he had driven the Hillman. Even though it was the first time with a trailer attached, Clark had taken the proper precautions when fastening the bar into the socket and tightening the lock screw with a spanner. The police could find no evidence of carelessness. A week later Frederick and Albert Mellers, well-respected members of the parish, were laid to rest side by side in a family grave in Epworth cemetery.

In the late 1940s, the town celebrated the exploits of Edwin Lindley, the 18-year-old son of Mr. J. E. and Mrs. Lindley of Laburnum House, Hollingsworth Lane. Edwin started playing football for Epworth Intermediates and, after a couple of matches with Epworth Town F.C., he went to play in Ashby. Spotted by scouts from Scunthorpe United and invited to trial, he played games at halfback and inside forward. His play impressed all to the point that he soon transferred to Nottingham Forest for a four-figure sum. His future as a professional footballer seemed assured. Two years later Edwin died in Scunthorpe Hospital from injuries sustained when his motorbike collided with another on Belgorthorne Hill. Members of the Observer Corps, on duty at the station, heard the noise of the collision and rushed to the scene. They found Edwin and Ernest Anguige lying unconscious in the road and arranged transport for both the injured men to be taken to Scunthorpe Hospital. Sadly, Edwin died there two days later. Ernest Anguige from The Grange, Beltoft Road, suffered a broken collarbone and other injuries but the hospital declared him 'comfortable.'

In January 1984, Hogarth Hill, to the north of Epworth, was slippery with mud as David Lindley drove his school bus towards the town. A well-known and popular farmer, David epitomised the natural bond between man and the land. Hardworking and committed, he had for many years helped transport pupils to and from South Axholme School. Approaching the hill, David was unaware of an out of control lorry slewing across the carriageway on the muddiest section of the road. The side of the truck hit the front of the bus, pinning David in the driver's cab. He died before help could reach him. At the inquest, the driver of the lorry stated that as he approached the bend in the road at about forty miles an hour, he lost control of the vehicle and was unable to correct the slide. The police reported that the mud on the road came from the tyres of lorries leaving the nearby brickworks. Although the company had a machine to clear the route of the sludgy mess they were unable to use it as the local authority would not grant a licence for its use on the public highway. The best the company could do was clean the entrance to the site and the unsurfaced road leading to the factory. The company last used the machine three days before the accident. The inquest heard that the police had to abandon skid tests to try to recreate the path of the lorry because doing this created too much danger. Within a few weeks of the accident, the local authority granted a licence for the sweeping machine, and the company hard surfaced the access road to try to limit the amount of mud lorries servicing the site transferred to the main carriageway.

In December 1695, James Middleton visited Abraham de la Pryme and told him the story of a servant from Wroot called John. A willing worker, John relied on his brawn and as such many regarded him as dim-witted. Middleton explained that about two months previously, John got it into his head that because his master paid him a pittance he could 'earn' more from robbing on the highway. When he told his master he would be leaving his employ the master asked him what job he would be taking up. John told him was going to be a 'padder.' Surprised by John's honesty, the master advised him against turning to robbery as an occupation. Despite this, the next morning, John set off on horseback with a large club in his hand.

On the London Road close to Grantham, John overtook someone he believed to be a gentleman. Slowing down, he allowed the gentleman to catch up with him whereupon he grabbed the man's bridle and bid him 'stand and deliver!' The man's reaction took John surprise as he threw open his hands and laughed. 'What is this?' he laughed, 'would a thief rob another thief, you are either a fool or you have never been at this trade before?'

When John acknowledged this to be true, the highwayman gave him sound advice. 'When you have mind to rob a man,' he said, 'never take hold of his bridle and bid him stand. First, knock him down and then you have him at your will.'

As they travelled on the highwayman passed on tips about his art. Eventually they came to a rough part of the road and John told the highwayman that as he knew the land well he would go ahead.

As he passed in front of the highwayman, John swung the club knocking his companion to the ground. 'Is that how you show your gratitude for the advice I gave you?' the highwayman called out. Ignoring the man's pleas, John clubbed him again. Having him at his mercy, John took all the money from the highwayman's pocket then swopped horses and galloped back to Wroot as fast as he could. There, despite arriving at the village with a new horse and a large sum of money, he asked for his old job back, telling his master that the life of a 'padder' was not for him!

During the eighteenth-century, highwaymen were said to be 'as common as crows,' and no one rode alone without fear of being robbed. For those travelling in the North Isle there was danger from two notable highwaymen, Ned Mandrell, said to have been a 'ruthless villain who was scared by none,' and Snowden Dunhill. Both operated in the area around Garthorpe; indeed Mandrell is thought to have been captured and hung; his remains being buried between Garthorpe and Luddington. Dunhill was sentenced to hard labour at York Assizes and transported to Tasmania, Australia. After serving his sentence and while awaiting transport back to England, Snowden Dunhill died. In Epworth, Thomas Cutforth was the one to avoid. Thomas' career ended when he was captured and sent to prison in Lincoln. It is believed that he was executed there in 1720. For many years a small ashlar limestone headstone with a segmental top could be seen six metres south-west of the chancel of Epworth Church. In memory of Thomas the words on the stone read: Honesty is ye best Thomas Cutforth I hope is gon to rest, March 27, 1720.

A hundred and eighty years later another 'highwayman story' caused quite a commotion in the villages of Eastoft and Luddington. Fourteen-year-old Alf Harrison, a farm labourer, turned up at his employer, Mr. Harrison, in a most distressed state. He claimed he had been set upon and robbed by a tall thin man with a thin

Thomas Cutforth's tombstone.

moustache. Mr. Harrison immediately called the police and it was not long before Inspector Peach arrived and began question the boy. Alf told him that he was walking home when a man sprang upon him and shouted, 'Your money or your life!' Taking hold of Alf 'by the scruff of the neck,' the man threw him to the ground and took four shillings from the boy's pocket. He then ran off down Dirty Lane. After further questioning Alf went on to describe the man's appearance – aged about thirty years, he wore an old black cap and black trousers with a hole 'in the nether part.' Round his neck he wore an old kerchief made from green material. His boots were dirty with 'the soles almost off.' His jacket sleeves were torn and he wore grey stockings. When Inspector Peach asked how he knew the stockings were grey, Alf told him, 'one of his stockings was turned down over his boot top.' When questioned about his clothes, Alf said that 'his coat was a bit mucky.' The intrepid inspector was becoming suspicious of the boy's story and he asked Alf to go and bring the coat. He found it clean, with no sign of mud on it. The inspector then asked Alf for the truth, and reminding of the story of George Washington and the tree, told him it would be a serious matter if he continued with the lie. The boy broke down in tears and admitted he never seen such a man and had not been knocked down or robbed. He confessed to spending the money on tobacco and inventing a story so his parents wouldn't find out. He said he had been reading 'Bloodthirsty Mike,' and 'The Roaming Ghostly Terror of the Black Rocky Isle,' and it was from these books he got the idea of being accosted by a highwayman. Inspector Peach gave him a severe reprimand and sent him off to explain to his parents. Unfortunately, before the truth of the 'robbery' reached the ears of the residents of the two villages, many refused to travel on the highway for fear of being confronted by a 'thin man with a thin moustache!'

CHAPTER FOUR

Hazards from Above

MISADVENTURE AND MYTH

In the early years of aviation, aircraft flying over the Isle were a rarity. In the year leading up to the First World War, the only recorded landing of an aircraft in the Isle was in 1823 when a hot air balloon, piloted by a Mr. Green, came down in the Park area of Westwoodside. As the craft neared the ground, Green threw out his landing ropes, and two men rushed forward to secure the balloon. As they helped Green alight the ropes snapped, and the balloon began to ascend leaving the poor pilot half-in and half-out. Not wishing to lose his precious craft, Green began to haul himself back into the basket. After a period of uncertainty and as the danger increased proportionately to the rise of the balloon, he finally tumbled inside. As the onlookers watched with a mixture of relief and apprehension, Green disappeared eastwards over Gainsborough. Carried off by an increasingly strong wind, Green fought to control the balloon as it headed out towards the coast. After hours of battling against the elements, he managed to bring the balloon down to the ground again on another 'Isle;' - the Island of Texel in the Netherlands!

Certainly, the landing of powered aircraft in the Isle was unheard of until 1916 when two aeroplanes were forced down on two consecutive days. Not surprisingly, the landings drew large crowds. The first aeroplane landed late in the day in the green fields at Low Melwood Farm owing to the pilot's inability to fly through a dense fog that clung to the land on either side of the River Trent. So great was the crowd that watched its departure the next day that those present seized the opportunity to organise a collection for the Red Cross Fund; raising the grand sum of £2. The following day another plane alighted at Sandtoft when the fog returned. It stayed there for three days and, when news spread that it, too, was about to leave, a large number of people turned up, 'as if from nowhere!'

Later in the summer, it was the turn of Lawns Farm to become an emergency aerodrome when a pilot, who had 'come down low to get his bearings,' was forced to land. Having done so safely, he found himself unable to restart the aeroplane's engine. Another plane with an engineer, sent to assist, was seen flying low over Thompson's Mill before locating the 'casualty.' The plane's problem could not be fixed until the following day so, members of the Volunteer Force mounted guard over the machines throughout the night. It was their most important task to date, and they relished the role. When the officers and engineer set off in search of somewhere to stay for the night, they were not short of offers from locals keen to have dashing aviators as their guests. Next day, news of the impending departure of both crafts drew a crowd of several hundred people who came to see the planes take off.

Although the Isle was not a target for air raids, Zeppelin airships did cross Lincolnshire and Nottinghamshire at night on their way to bomb some of the larger northern towns. These very observable structures, and a media that tended to blow out of proportion the danger they posed, caused a mixture of curiosity (some people would gaze as though transfixed at the imposing sight of these floating monsters), and alarm throughout Axholme. Indeed there was consternation in the Graizelound to Owston Ferry area when reports began to circulate of people hearing the whirring sound of Zeppelin engines on spring evenings. The reports confused the authorities who could find no evidence of these structures being in the area. Eventually, investigations revealed the sounds came from a colony of male frogs advertising themselves to potential partners!

Later in the year, on the night of Saturday 2 September 1916, the Isle suffered its nearest raid as Zeppelin L-13 crossed East Stockwith and dropped a number of bombs on the village. There was slight damage to a few cottages but no loss of life (except for a few pheasants in the woods and fields). Eight-year-old Sydney Stephenson and his brother Leslie, however, were trapped in their home by falling timbers and felt themselves lucky to survive. Their sister, Nellie, so traumatised by the ordeal fled into the fields and went 'missing' for several days. In its report on the raid, the Nottingham Daily said the Zeppelin departed the area 'at great altitude and terrific speed.' Reports elsewhere spoke of apples being 'baked on the trees and roosting wild birds roasted alive.' One bomb that fell in a field but did not explode became the object 'of much interest,' being, 'half buried in the ground, with its handle protruding.' The children of East Stockwith spent their free time roaming the district collecting pieces of shrapnel, and there were reports of busloads of 'tourists' coming to the village to view the 'devastation!' Some enterprising youngsters even sought to increase their pocket money by selling bits of recovered metal.

It was in January 1931, however, that the 'greatest' air accident happened in the Isle. On a dark Monday night, with the Isle covered in its customary winter mist, the pilots of three Army planes, flying from Northampton to RAF Digby, became unaware of their whereabouts and decided to descend from the dark sky overhead to look for a suitable place to land. It was almost impossible to see the character of the land below but they knew the ground would be relatively flat and this would give them a fair chance of performing a successful crash landing. One large machine, a Vickers Vimy twin bomber, with a crew of four men, crashed on the roadway near Park Drain Station, tore through a hedge, flipped across a dyke and ended upside down in a field. Three of the crew in the front of the plane died instantly; the fourth, Aircraftsman Cecil Jones, though seriously injured, managed to scramble out from the rear section of the plane.

The second machine landed safely some way ahead. The third just missed the postman cycling along the road and crashed into a telegraph pole, dragging it over a hundred yards across a ploughed field. Two men from this plane were injured though not seriously. Patrons of the Park Drain Hotel and railway workers from Park Drain station rushed across the fields to render first aid, and the pilot of the third plane soon found himself in an ambulance bound for Doncaster Royal Infirmary.

Removing the bodies from the Vickers proved too difficult in the darkness, so a constable was placed on guard duty overnight. Shortly before midnight, however, a party of airmen arrived from RAF Digby to take over guarding the plane. Next day came the grisly task of removing the bodies. The military authorities did this behind screens in a fenced off area of the field - the public being kept well back from the activity.

At the inquest, Aircraftsman Jones described his thrilling escape from death, as the plane pancaked on to its resting place in the field. 'We were flying very low,' he said, 'to see the name of the station here. We ascended again, circled round, and prepared for a forced landing. We tried to get down in a green field by the side of the station. We apparently overshot this field and landed in a ploughed field. We ran along the bank and then struck a dyke. What happened next I don't know. I could see the dyke. The machine seemed to go up in the air and then straight on to its nose. It partly overturned and crushed those in front. I escaped through being in the cockpit at the back. If the dyke had not been there, the accident would not have happened.' Returning a verdict of 'death from misadventure,' the coroner replied that, unfortunately, this being the Isle of Axholme 'the place was full of dykes!'

On Christmas Eve 1944, forty-five V1 rockets, aimed at Manchester, fell across a broad swathe of land in the North of England. The missiles were air-launched between 0500hrs and 0600hrs from modified Heinkels of Squadron KG53, approximately forty miles off the East Coast between Hornsea and Mablethorpe. A fisherman in the North Sea witnessed the launch and reported that some of the rockets failed to ignite and fell harmlessly into the sea. The RAF radar station at Lowestoft picked up the raid and alerted the defences along the coast, but anti-aircraft gunners failed to destroy any of the incoming rockets. Although these 'doodlebugs' fired from Heinkels were notoriously inaccurate, some thirty-one rockets reached the target area with fifteen falling on Manchester, killing thirty-five people. The missile spread, however, was considerable, stretching from Spennymoor in County Durham to Newport in Shropshire. One of the stray doodlebugs fell on Epworth, landing close to Thompson's Mill. The resulting blast blew out the large shop windows in the Market Place but left the smaller ones intact. There is one eyewitness account of the doodlebug from children watching what they took to be 'a small plane with flames shooting out of the tail' (though what young children were doing out so early makes one question the validity of the report). Apparently, the engine cut out but, after a few seconds, started up again and carried the rocket on for another two miles before it fell. Had the engine fired up a second or two later there is a real prospect that rocket could have landed in the middle of Epworth causing considerable damage and bringing death to the town.

The Doodlebug incident was just one of a large number of aircraft incidents over the Isle during World War Two. On the third of April 1942, two Spitfires from 133 Squadron collided over Epworth and came down in the surrounding fields. Both American pilots ejected successfully; Pilot Officer W.A. Arends landed safely but the parachute of Pilot Officer S.F. Whedon failed to deploy, and he was killed on impact with the ground. A few months later, a Tiger Moth crash landed in Crowle while practising low flying. Both pilots emerged from the wreckage unhurt. Two years later, the pilot of a Halifax, three minutes from take-off at RAF Sandtoft, lost control in a banking manoeuvre over Crowle. This caused the plane to crash land from two hundred feet but fortunately neither the airmen nor the residents of Crowle suffered. The occupants of a cottage in Belton had a near miss when a Halifax, landing awkwardly, crashed into the building. Fortunately, no one suffered serious injury, though all six crew had to be treated for minor cuts and bruises. In other near misses in the Isle, a Polish Spitfire pilot crashed at Monkham Bridge Farm, Westwoodside when his fuel line failed in flight; a Hampden came down over Owston Ferry when the pilot, dazzled by searchlights, lost his bearings

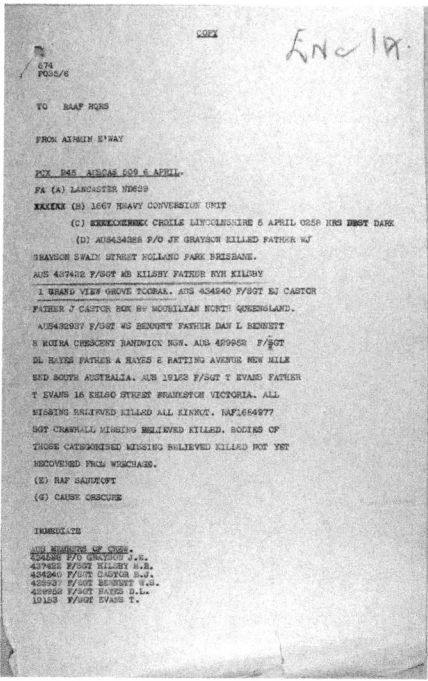

Record of the Lancaster crash at Crowle on 5 April 1945.

and another Halifax, returning to RAF Sandtoft with a damaged engine crashed in a field close to Epworth. Six men from RAF Blyton were killed when their aircraft crashed near Haxey after the pilot took evasive action to avoid colliding with a Spitfire. The early months of 1945, however, brought servicemen deaths to the Isle on an unprecedented scale. On 5 April Lancaster ND639 crashed at Crowle while undertaking a 'Bullseye' operation killing seven of the crew. Ten days later, Lancaster PB565, thirty minutes into a cross-country training flight nose-dived towards ground at Owston Ferry. As the angle of the dive increased, the aircraft broke up before impact. None of the crew survived the crash!

Opened in February 1944, RAF Sandtoft became a training base for pilots of Lancaster and Halifax bombers. The base saw so many crashes that it was nicknamed 'Prangtoft.' There were examples of planes hitting planes taxying on the runway, planes coming in to land colliding overhead with those taking off and others overshooting the runway or slewing to either side. Several accidents were due to the inexperience of the pilot but there was a number caused by aircraft malfunctions such as tyres bursting on impact with the ground and undercarriages collapsing. After its third mechanical failure, trainee pilots refused to fly Halifax DG338 resulting in it being 'retired' from service. In one 'overshoot,' on 30 October 1944, Halifax LL226 careered off the runway and ploughed into the bungalow owned by Mr. and Mrs. Wraith, killing the pilot, both the occupants and a passing cyclist, Mr. T. S. Nixon. After the War, the airfield was placed on care and maintenance and remained inactive until allocated to the United States Air Force on 1 April 1953. However, the USAF never occupied the station, and it reverted to Ministry of Defence control on 8 September 1955. Put up for disposal, parts of the airfield were sold in 1968. Today it has been converted to industrial and agricultural use and houses a trolley bus museum and a flying club that uses one of the taxi tracks as a runway.

Further west, Lindholme was the base for Wellington Bombers and figured significantly in the operations over Germany. Ostensibly a Royal Airforce Base, it housed a squadron of Polish airman, whose thirst for avenging the atrocities committed on their nation bordered on the manic. Some seemed to thrive on a perilous lifestyle that threatened their well-being. Throughout the war, Polish crews were noted for their dedication and efficiency but it was their willingness to fly, even when having just come back from an exhausting raid, that personified their fanatic desire to engage with the enemy. Perhaps their desire to be 'in the air' stemmed from their hatred of Axholme mists and the food, in particular, custard which they likened to the yellow past of washing powder. They were, however, attracted to the local girls, and their attention captivated many young ladies who would go 'weak at the knees' at the sight of these romantic and attentive airmen.

The squadron's first operational mission took place on 23 July 1941 when eight aircraft attacked Frankfurt. The Polish crews' willingness to fly long and dangerous missions saw them return utterly exhausted and this ultimately led to the demise of one plane and all of its occupants. At 1.30 p.m., on 27 September 1941, the crew of Wellington W5557 were on their approach to land at Lindholme in poor visibility. At the controls, the pilot, bleeding profusely from wounds sustained in the attack struggled to keep control. Realising a safe landing might not be possible, the crew prepared for the worst. The bomber overshot the runway and crashed into the boggy ground beyond, killing all four members of its Polish crew.

Some weeks later the station chaplain reported an encounter with a bloodstained pilot who asked for directions to the officers' mess. Somewhat alarmed by the state of the pilot, the chaplain pointed in the direction of the crew's quarters, and before he could offer any further assistance, the man walked off and disappeared into the darkness. Later, when the chaplain enquired as to the health of the wounded pilot, no one knew anything about him. It was the first of many subsequent sightings that tell of a ghostly pilot roaming the moors in search of his lost crew and asking strangers directions to the officers' mess. Other stories speak of the ghost appearing in the night, often beside the bed of the pilots. On one occasion, a pilot so shocked by the apparition, let out a scream that woke the whole dormitory. The base converted to a prison in 1985 and for a while there are accounts of prisoners experiencing ghostly apparitions in the cells.

After the war, the base remained active, and one night a mechanic working late was so scared by an encounter with the 'ghost' that he left his post. When reporting on a charge of dereliction of duty to his commanding officer he spoke of seeing a man dressed in what appeared to be a Second World War flying suit 'talking in a foreign tongue.' In 1962, a witness recalled walking across the deserted airfield with a friend and seeing a light in the derelict control tower. Both knew that the building should have been empty. Closing on the hanger area, they were suddenly surrounded by sounds of activity. They could hear the screech of hanger doors opening, the whir of aircraft engines starting and the patter of feet running to and from the building. When they reached the hangar, to their horror, there was nothing to see. Some years later, Lieutenant Colonel Stephen Jenkins and an RAF squadron leader returning from a training course at nearby RAF Finningley reported seeing a figure dressed in a flying kit, standing near the spot where the Polish bomber crashed. It was even said that the distinctive tail of the aircraft could sometimes be seen rising and sinking again when the ghost was on the prowl.

One evening, in what he termed 'the gloaming,' Harold Woolgar along with his wife Win were on their way to the Green Tree Pub for a meal. As their car left Sandtoft, the headlights picked out the figure of a man at the side of the road who they thought was 'thumbing a lift.' Pulling up alongside the figure, Harold wound down the window and asked if he could help. The figure (which Harold noted was wearing a forage cap) leaned towards the car and said, 'Tell me the way to the sick quarters.' Harold questioned the man as to which 'sick quarters' he was referring. At this point, the figure vanished and could no longer be seen in the headlights. The couple continued their journey to the Green Tree and sometime later recounted the story. They were amazed to hear the stories about the 'ghost' pilot of Lindholme.

While peat cutting on 23 July 1987, a local farmer unearthed the corpse of a forty-six-year-old Polish airman some nine feet down in the peat. When he notified the Polish authorities he reported the body as being 'perfectly preserved.' They arrived to take the body away. Burial took place with full military honours in a cemetery at Newark. From that day there have been no more

Camera trickery shows the 'lost' airmen (photogtaph courtesy of Harold Woolgar).

sightings of the spirit that locals nicknamed 'Lindholme Willy,' 'Billy Lindholme' or 'Pete the Pole.'

However just maybe on a cold, bright winter night when the moon creates bizarre shadows across the desolate moors on the western borders of North Lincolnshire, should your eye catch a curious movement, you may recall the story of the 'lost' airman and wonder....!

In 1953 a Meteor Jet crashed in a field at Low Burnham, narrowly missing three generations of the Smith family who were at work in the fields. The pilot, Flight-Lieutenant Tanbred, was killed outright in what was thought to be his attempts to avoid the plane coming down over Haxey. In 2003, fifty years to the day after the crash, family members came to the crash site to meet John Smith one of those in the fields that day. After a short service of remembrance, the family laid a wreath at the spot where the plane came down.

No exploration of incidents in the sky over Axholme would be complete without a good Unidentified Flying Object story. On New Year's Eve 1978, residents in Westwoodside waiting to go to a New Year Party, spotted a brilliant glow in the sky, travelling in a northerly direction. The object appeared to be moving at a slow but constant speed and had a 'tail' stretching out behind it. One witness described the phenomenon as being, 'so clear that it looked like a train with carriages lit up. In fact, it looked close enough to pick out individual windows.' After watching the glowing light for some time, it disappeared from their view over the rooftops. Baffled, excited and a little fearful, the onlookers went to the party and told those there of their experience. Some days later, the U.K. UFO Spotting Agency responded to other reports of the strange lights in the sky by confirming they came from a part of an old rocket burning up as it entered the earth's atmosphere.

Finally, in this exploration of danger from the skies over Axholme, we return to the early nineteenth-century and explore one incident from the eccentric life of John Hall. Described in the Epworth Bells many years later as 'an inventive genius,' John owned a mill that stood close to the church in Epworth. One of his more eccentric ideas was a long held the belief that one day he would fly. To this end, and much in the same way as Leonardo da Vinci, he studied the flight of birds and concluded that with a properly constructed pair of wings and sufficient height he could propel himself through the air.

On the day of his 'maiden flight,' he struggled to the balcony around the top of his mill dragging a pair of wooden framed, canvas wings behind him. As he teetered on the edge, those in the crowd who came to support him offered words of encouragement. They had been party to the success of some of his less madcap schemes and were firmly of the opinion that if anyone could do it, John could! Others were more sceptical, and several agreed they expected John 'to drop like a stoan!' Sadly, but predictably, it was the latter view that proved correct as John launched himself into the air and despite flapping furiously, he did indeed 'drop like a stone.'

Fearing the worst, his friends, along with those who regarded the attempt as foolhardy, rushed towards the fractured mass of canvas and wood only to find John struggling to free himself from the mess he had created. Bruised and shaken but otherwise free from severe injury they helped him to his feet. To spare his feelings over his failure they declared his attempt to be 'a creditable performance.' John, however, was far from downhearted and claimed his efforts a success. He argued that without the help of the wings that had not created uplift but had slowed his descent, his injuries could have been far worse! He left the scene vowing to make improvements to the structures, confident that his next attempt would be more successful. There are, however, no records of him experimenting further in aviation. Considering his experience, the report in the Epworth Bells was, perhaps, a little premature in lauding him as 'one of the first man-flyers.'

CHAPTER FIVE

Moorland Myths

FOLKLORE AND ILLUSION

On the afternoon of 1 June 1747, John Tate, a labouring man, digging for peat on the moors surrounding the village of Amcotts, cut through the foot of a woman buried in the fen. Having dug to a depth of six feet and seeing the partial remains of the foot encased in a sandal, he ran from the scene terrified. Sometime later, Dr. George Stovin of Hirst Priory, hearing of the discovery determined to finish the excavation and set off with his gardener, Thomas Perfect and some others to find the place. They found the sandal soon after arriving at the scene with the bones and gristle of the feet in it, and further digging revealed a second sandal. Stovin likened them to moccasins made from one whole piece of rawhide, with only one short seam at the heel. The sandals had five loops cut in the leather on each side, and ten small loops at the toe. They were laced up along the top of the foot, with a thong of the same leather. This system enabled the wearer to draw up the toe like the mouth of a purse. As he excavated further, Stovin found the thigh bones and the skin of the lower parts of the body with fresh hair on it. It was the body of a woman lying on its side.

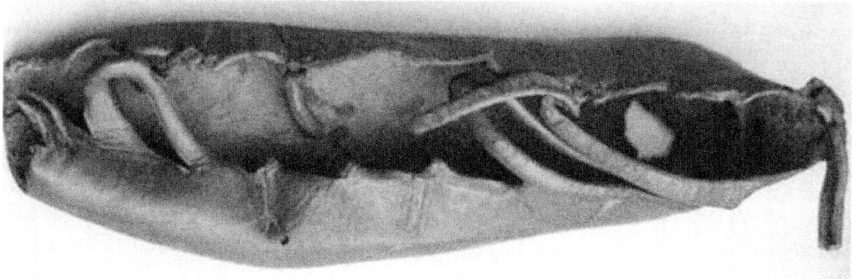

The Amcotts' Sandal.

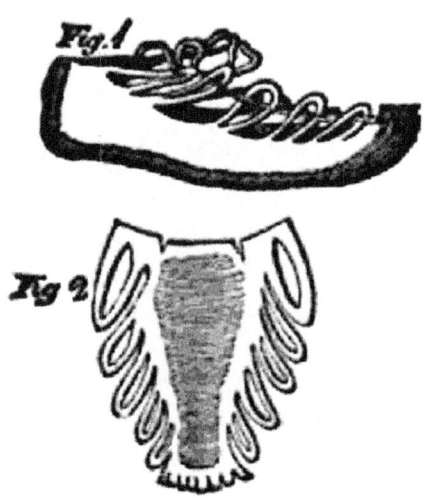

Detail of the sandal showing the loop fasteners.

The men worked their way along the trench and came across the skin of an arm and a hand, with well-preserved fingernails that Stovin described as being 'firm and fast on the fingers as fresh as any person living.' He recorded the woman's body as bent, with her head and feet close to touching. He described the skin of the corpse as 'strong.' Apart from the arm and hand, and the tawny coloured sandals, Stovin took the remains of the woman to Amcotts' chapel yard where he buried them. After showing the hand and sandal to his 'worthy friend' Thomas Whichcot, of Harpswell, Knight of the Shire for the County of Lincoln in Parliament, who somewhat surprisingly tried on the sandal on his foot, he sent them to the Royal Society in London. Members here concluded that the objects dated from a time earlier than Edward IV, but not before the time of Edward I or Henry III when shoes

George Stovin born about 1695 or 1696 was an antiquarian and author of the Stovin manuscript. He led the life of a country gentleman, which allowed him the opportunity to follow the topographical and antiquarian researches which from his early years he found fascinating. His father and his other older relations must have passed on many curious tales from the time of the drainage and of life on the meres, marshes and swamps.

of this fashion first became worn. Their estimate was incorrect by about a thousand years as subsequent investigations placed the sandal in the late Roman period - A.D. 200 - 400. There being no apparent signs of burial, logic dictated that the woman had perished on the marshy plain having lost her way amid the desolate landscape, though some suggested that the woman may have been sacrificed to appease the gods.* Some ten years after Stovin's find, William Biddy of Thorne, out digging turf on the moor, found the entire body of a man with firm teeth and hair. The body had skin that resembled tanned leather, dyed yellowish by the peat-stained waters of the moor. Since then no other bodies have come to light in the area, but the tantalising prospect remains that there may be others out there just awaiting discovery.

Abraham de la Pryme** speaks of an old hall that stood empty on an area known to this day as the Levels. He wrote about the many dreadful tales and disturbances caused by witches and spirits in this most dreadful of all places. One tale that takes many forms, and a 'story' familiar to many Isle folk was that of William (Billy) Lindholme. De la Pryme records William as a cunning hermit, wearing strange skins and turning the fur to the inside. Beneath this, he wore a tunic fastened round his body with a rope made from reeds. According to de la Pryme, he lived in a humble, lonesome cell, free from care and noise and 'neither pomp, pride, nor cursed strife disturbed the quiet of his life.'

Some people suggested that Billy could command the marsh goblins and sprites to do his will. George Stovin who visited

---

In 2017 the sandal went on display at Scunthorpe museum.

**Abraham de la Pryme, the son of Matthias de la Pryme and Sarah Smague (or Smagge) was born at Hatfield in 1671 and christened at Sandtoft French Protestant Chapel. Along with his duties as a local curate he devoted much of his time to natural history, chemistry and even dabbled in magic. He died at the age of 34, after visiting the sick. He was buried in Hatfield church. From the age of 12 he kept a diary. This and his 'History of Hatfield Chase' provide a valuable insight into life in the area around North Lincolnshire.*

Lindholme in 1727 with the Reverend Samuel Wesley set out much of the story in a letter to the Gentleman's Magazine. He wrote, 'The people of Hatfield and places adjacent have a tradition that in the middle of Hatfield waste there formerly lived an ancient hermit who was called William of Lindholme; he was by the common people taken for a cunning man or conjurer, but in order to be better informed I, accompanied by the Rev'd Mr. Sam Wesley and others, went to view the place and, after passing the morass, found the hermitage or cell situate in the middle of sixty acres of firm sandy ground full of pebbles on which was growing barley, oats and peas. There was likewise a well four or five yards deep full of clear spring water which is very remarkable because the water of the morass is the colour of coffee. Here is a great plenty of furze bushes, etc, and a variety of game such as hares, foxes, kites, eagles, curlews, ducks and geese; there is no house or cottage near it, and but a few old oaks, willows and birch; the house is a little stud-bound one, and seems ready to fall. At the east stood an altar made of hewn stone, and at the west is the hermit's grave covered with a large free stone that measures in length eight foot and a half, in breadth three feet, and in thickness eight inches, which, with the consent of Richard Holgate, the present inhabitant and the help of levers, were raised up and removed, and, digging under found a tooth, a skull, the thigh and shin bones of a human body, all of a very large size; we likewise found in the grave a peck of hempseed and a beaten piece of copper.' On the large stone was an inscription which those present could not decipher. Later on, locals broke the stone into pieces to use them as rubbing stones, nullifying any chance of ever revealing the words carved into its surface.

In another excavation in 1869, when the time came for a new farmhouse on Lindholme, a Mr. Wright removed the old building called the Hermitage. Under the floor, he found a large stone, seven feet six inches long, four feet broad and nine inches thick, neatly dressed by a mason's chisel. Beneath the stone, he found a brick vault with a skull and the leg and arm bones of a human.

Another version of the tale has William as a giant lad, much put upon by his father. Supposedly taking advantage of the lad's strength, which came from him being in league with 'infernal spirits,' his father made him do all the heavy work on the farm. One story tells of William going to a neighbouring farm to fetch some straw. When they could not agree upon a specific amount the farmer told him to take as much as he could carry, William thrust his fork into a haystack, hefted it on to his shoulders and walked home with it on his back! On the surface this sounds implausible but one has to remember that haystacks at that time were nothing like the 'house size' constructions of a few years back.

Resenting being put upon by his parents, however, William's anger rose to the point that he attempted to kill them by hurling a massive boulder after them as they left home to go to Wroot Feast. The stone missed but became so embedded in the ground that no human could move it. Legend has it that six farm horses were brought in to remove the boulder but the task was too much, and all six fell dead with exhaustion. Stories that the stone was cursed spread around the district and it was never disturbed again. Locals said, '... no one da-ares so much as ter touch the stoo-an, or terra-rise it noo, though its nearly gressed o'er. If iver it should get gressed o'er then, th' earth'll be covered wi' blood! No moss'll grow on t' stoo-an, for t' stoo-an eats it off as fast as it grows.' There were two other stones in the area supposedly thrown by William; one the locals called the 'thumb stone' and the other the 'little finger stone.' For several years, many believed ill luck would befall anyone meddling with these. There are no ancient records of a religious building on Lindholme, but what is beyond doubt is that someone lived, died and was buried there. Saintly hermit, jealous murderer or resentful giant .... ? The stories are best left in the past.

There is little doubt that, although the locals sought to live with and adapt the landscape where possible, they feared its unpredictability. From early times, venturing out onto the Axholme marshes was a dangerous undertaking. The paths through the 'fenny land' were often complex, and failure to reach a dwelling before dark would likely fill the superstitious peasant with apprehension and misgiving. A self-igniting gas present on the fenny parts of the Isle, known as ignis fatuus, often appeared on the surface of the water as a small flickering flame. To the unsuspecting traveller, this light might have appeared as a lantern held by a dusky figure. Locals called this phenomenon Will o' the Wisp and believed it to be one of the faerie folk of the fens who, carrying a light to lead the way, entices a wayfarer off the path and in the darkness lures them on to certain death in the marshscape. Transfixed to the point of being hypnotised by the light, the traveller follows its meandering path and finds himself lost in the watery wastes. It is at this precise moment that the lantern-carrier lifts the light high above its head, lets out a malicious laugh and extinguishes the flame. Disoriented, lost and a long way from home, the poor traveller is left standing in pitch darkness with little chance of finding a safe route out of the hostile landscape. Folklore dictated that the safest thing to do when these dancing lights appeared, was to ignore their hypnotic effect and make for the nearest shelter. If there was no safe place nearby, the most prudent action to take was to lie face down until the lights vanished.

This familiar and cautionary tale concerning the phenomenon held sway for many, however, ignis fatuus was not always considered dangerous. Some tales have Will-o'-the-Wisp as the guardian of treasure, leading those brave enough to follow to sure riches. Other stories tell of travellers getting lost, and having treated the spirit with kindness and consideration, found he would guide them to safety.

An equally evil creature was the boggart, a malevolent and shape-shifting genius that lived outdoors in the marshy land; in holes in the ground; under bridges and on dangerous sharp bends in the road. More than just a nuisance, these stocky dwarf-like beings often appeared to foretell death. Some believed them to be the souls of stillborn infants bound for revenge. If someone lost on the mired land was never seen again, Islonians claimed they had been caught and devoured by a marsh boggart. Surly, unpredictable, mean and very difficult to appease, there were also boggarts that lived in the household and brought mischief to a family, stealing food and hiding household items like keys and socks. So attached to the family were these mischievous spirits that many believed they followed their 'folk' from home to home and in many a house, often close by the fire, the home dweller would leave a small seat on which the boggart could find rest and warmth during the night. Other examples of their mischief included: crawling into people's beds at night; blowing out candles; putting a sweaty hand on faces and even pulling on a person's ears. Remedies to ward off boggarts included hanging a horseshoe on the front door of the house or leaving a pile of salt outside the bedroom. As with Will-o'-the-Wisp, some claimed boggarts could be pacified by flattery, by acts of kindness, and, in some cases by gracious acceptance.

Long before the Dutch drained the marshland, a race of small pixie folk lived in the Axholme wetlands. These creatures, supposedly no taller than a hand's span, were called 'Tiddy,' a reference perhaps to their tiny size or a derivation of the expression 'tide-y,' as these beings were believed to control the inrush of water from the rivers. Capricious by nature they were neither good nor evil. Some folk maintained they helped crops grow and pinched open the buds of flowering plants in the spring. The ruler of these miniature folk and the chief guardian of the fenland was Tiddy Mun (Little Man), a being somewhat larger than his subjects. He inhabited the water holes of the slimy morass and, as the damp mist rose over the 'fenny land' he moved unseen among the locals, his long, mousy hair hanging erratically about his drab, wizened face.

Tiddy Mun - drawing by Jo Meays.

If in times of flood, the locals heard the sound of running water and saw the water levels rise around the villages, they would go out into night and call 'Tiddy Mun wi'out a name, tha watters thruff!' ('Tiddy Mun without a name, the water's through!'). They would keep reciting this chorus until they heard the cry of the peewit, supposedly the accepting response of Tiddy Mun. The next morning when the villagers woke they expected to find the water levels abating. When Cornelius Vermuyden arrived to drain the Isle, it is said that Tiddy Mun became so angry at the change to the local landscape he laid a curse on the land – ponies became lame, cattle became sick and lambs and pigs died. Worst of all disease came to the children. As the old rural ways in Axholme disappeared and a more modern agricultural system developed, the Tiddy folk could no longer determine the landscape and they disappeared. The last to leave was Tiddy Mun himself never to be seen or heard again.

Until 1863, when Borley Rectory took on the mantle of the most haunted house in England, the Rectory at Epworth held that dubious title. Supposedly, between 2 December 1716 and 31 January 1717, the rectory was subjected to poltergeist activity on an unprecedented scale. The day-to-day accounts of several family members spoke of strange noises and unexplained incidents. Susanna Wesley reported seeing an apparition 'like a badger but without a head.' A servant described it more like a rabbit than a badger and others reported hearing sounds like the gobbling of a turkey. On other occasions invisible hands pushed people around; the accompanying noises resembling the turning of a mill, the crashing of a hundred bottles or the emptying of a bag of money over a table. The situation became worse when door latches lifted by themselves and even though one of the children tried to hold them down it proved impossible to do so. The noises were often preceded by howling from the family dog who would tremble and then creep away to hide beneath furniture. So incensed was Samuel that on one occasion he pulled a pistol from his belt threatening to kill the 'ghost' if it did not stop its knocking. The family referred to the entity as 'Old Jeffrey.'

Andrew Lang, a man much interested in ghost stories and someone who collected them assiduously, came to Epworth as a guest of Canon Overton in the 1880s, ostensibly to investigate the matter. Termed as a man of the Scottish Renaissance Lang contributed to academic works of poetry, fiction, and non-fiction. He became a noted collector of folk tales and sought insight into the role that dreams and supernatural elements play in folklore and myth.

*Old Jeffrey's chamber in Epworth Rectory.
From a drawing in the Methodist Recorder.*

He set out to interview some of the older inhabitants of the town to establish the validity of the stories. For a period it seems he held the opinion that Hetty Wesley caused the ghostly happenings. It was a view upheld by the American psychologist H. Addington Bruce. In 1908 Bruce saw discrepancies in the family's reports over time and believed it was the fallibility of human memory that led to an exaggeration of the experiences.

In late Victorian times, there were fears 'Old Jeffrey' was making his presence felt again; not in the Rectory this time but in a newly built house known to this day as 'The Gables.' When the Isle of Axholme Rural District Council decided to make some minor adjustments, the night watchman reported hearing knocking and spinning noises and felt a hand on his back. His description resembled closely those attributed to 'Old Jeffrey' by the Wesley family and led to the theory that their ghost had found a new home. On closer investigation, the watchman could find no physical cause for the noises and neither could those who agreed to look into his allegations.

That the Isle has its fair share of ghosts and ghostly happenings is beyond dispute. At some point in their ministry, many of the Isle's parish priests have been approached by people seeking an explanation of things outside their usual experience. Some years ago the Bishop of Lincoln advised the clergy of the Diocese, if required, to try to discern whether the thing that was 'going bump' was in the person's home or their head. In most cases, when sitting down with those afflicted, the priest was able to bring rational thought to the problem and although not performing exorcisms in the accepted sense, provided a conduit through which the sufferer could find their own solution. When called upon, the reasoning of a calm, quiet, undramatic, prayerful approach invariably ended the difficult experience. However, many priests accept that human beings are complex organisms and for many, the electric impulses created in our brains, strengthens a belief that we are more than just physical entities. As such, we seem to be part of a process that we do not fully understand. It may be that 'ghosts in our lives' enter some spiritual void and, however irrational, fill this zone of confusion. However fanciful they may seem, the tales below that tell of the experiences of people and 'things that go bump,' are well documented.

Legend has it that about two hundred years ago on St. Mark's Eve (24 April), a night set aside so that curious people could see who might die in the future, two men camped in the south porch of Haxey Church beneath a shining moon. The object of their vigil was to confirm a long-held belief that a procession of the phantoms of those due to die in the following twelve months would manifest themselves by entering then leaving the church during the night. The watchers knew they had to remain silent for two hours from when the church clock struck eleven o'clock. Having first performed the usual ceremonies and superstitions, they seated themselves, but after a while, when no apparitions appeared, they resolved to leave. However, both men seemed to be held fast by an overpowering force that left them unable to move their feet. Accepting they would have to sit out the allotted time of their vigil, both men settled back down. Soon after one of the men fell asleep. Almost immediately, through the inky blackness, a series of ghostly manifestations appeared, many quite indistinct, some wrapped in winding sheets and others who resembled friends and neighbours. Led by the ghostly manifestation of a minister, the phantoms (that seemed to radiate an inner light) approached the church, whereupon the doors flew open, allowing the ghostly figures to pass inside. There then came a noise resembling the rattling of bones and sound of earth being thrown into an open grave.

The apparition that caused the remaining watcher the greatest alarm, however, was the spectre of the friend asleep at his side. It was a chilling sight and one that disturbed the onlooker greatly. When the spectacle was over his friend awoke and asked if he had seen anything. Unable to disclose the sights he had seen he shrugged his shoulders and reported nothing. He kept this secret for months until one day, to his horror, he received a message to say his friend had died in an accident the night before. Chastened, the man believed for the rest of his life that, had he told his friend he knew of his impending death, he may have been able to avert it. Thankfully, the custom seems to have died out in the 1800s when rational thought outstripped aberrant superstition. The custom can be found in part of a long poem entitled, 'The Vigil of St. Mark' by James Montgomery. The relevant section reads –

'Tis now,' replied the village belle,
'St. Mark's mysterious eve,
And all that old traditions tell,
I tremblingly believe;
How, when the midnight signal tolls,
Along the churchyard green,

A mournful train of sentenced souls
In winding-sheets are seen.
The ghosts of all whom death shall doom
Within the coming year,
In pale procession walk the gloom,
Amid the silence drear.'

Just over the hill from Haxey, in the Brethergate area of neighbouring Westwoodside, legend tells of a headless female who walked the village lanes. Those who saw the apparition spoke of the female wandering aimlessly and casting about as though searching for something. It did not take a great leap of imagination for them to deduce that the spectre was searching for her lost head. Similarly, in the late nineteenth century, a bend of the Trent at Owston Ferry was supposedly haunted by Jenny Hearn. Resembling a small woman with the face of a seal and with long wavy hair that fell across the eyes this creature travelled on the water in a large pie dish using spoons as oars.

Further down the Trent at Keadby, two people walking close to the old, stone bridge spotted a man leaning over the parapet staring into the water below. As they moved closer and called for the man to take care, the figure vanished – as though 'in the blink of an eye.' They described the man as about six feet tall in a beige raincoat and a brimmed hat. Initially thinking the man had thrown himself into the water, they rushed to the point where they believed he entered the water. Arriving a few seconds later, they expected to see evidence of a body in the water – there was none. It was one of a number of 'sightings' that described a disappearing figure which continued until the bridge fell into disrepair being replaced by the present bascule bridge in 1916.

The December 1953 edition of the Yorkshire Post carried what was believed to be an Epworth ghost story. Late at night, some fifty residents of Epworth reported to the police that they heard ghostly sounds and what they took to be the words 'Save me' and 'Help' in the newly constructed housing estate of Coronation Crescent and Fieldside. When the police arrived they instigated a thorough search, combing the fields and moorlands with help from farmers who shone their tractor headlights into the gloomy landscape. They found nothing, and recorded the incident as 'unexplained.' Some weeks later they revisited the case and came up with a rational explanation; the noises were nothing more than the very loud and high-pitched scream of dog foxes which can be mistaken for the sound of a human crying for help.

There are many accounts of unexplained happenings in Epworth, from strangers in black inhabiting empty houses to the noises at the Rectory during Samuel Wesley's occupancy. One little-known story involves incidents that took place at what used to be Jack Stamp's bakery at the top of Pashley Walk. Allegedly the bakery was haunted by a spirit that the workers referred to as 'Nellie.' This 'presence' would fling tiles across the room, move candlesticks on the mantlepiece and take curd tarts from the counter. It was 'Nellie' who took the blame when a large upstairs mirror fell from its position on the wall and broke into a myriad of pieces. The mirror was so heavy that no single person could lift it. When the staff saw the devastation, their first thought was that it had fallen but the hook in the wall was as solid as ever, and the thick chain from which the mirror hung remained intact. There seemed only one rational explanation - someone, or something, with greater power than the average human must have dropped the mirror while trying to take it down from its wall bracket. On other occasions, as staff left the shop by car, the back door would open, then close of its own volition. This happened so often to not be a coincidence leaving the occupants to conclude that 'Nellie' had joined them for the forthcoming journey!

When Hannah Mary Pettinger was born at Sandhill Farm on Epworth Turbary in 1880, the doctor noted something strange. Hannah entered the world with part of the amniotic sack over her face - a condition known as a birth caul but sometimes referred to as a birth helmet or birth veil. It is not a dangerous condition but rare enough for it to happen once in eighty-thousand births. Such a rarity invariably attracted superstitions, and from the outset, Hannah was seen as 'special.' Her parents believed she would be a lucky child and immune from drowning for the rest of her life as long as she kept the caul safe. They placed the caul between two sheets of paper and told her to keep it safe. Hannah did so throughout her life, and she carried the title 'caul bearer' to her grave.

Tradition has it that caul bearers have, what might be called, 'peculiar abilities' and such was the case with Hannah. When the family moved to live on Belton Road, six-year-old Hannah caused consternation one day when she ran home claiming to have seen a man in what was the empty house next door. She described the man as wearing black, with a wide-brimmed hat and a beard. Her description was that of a Quaker who had died in the house some sixty-years ago! The daughter of a farmer and small in stature, in adulthood Hannah developed the ability of second sight. She could discern where there might be underground water and proved to be an effective judge of people's character and abilities. She had an uncanny ability to predict the weather, and local farmers often sought her advice when might be the best time to plant their crops.

Some say that as a caul bearer approaches death, the caul changes from its brittle state and becomes moist and pliable similar to its condition at birth. At the age of seventy-seven Hannah suffered a stroke. Fearing the worst, her daughter opened the drawer where Hannah kept the caul and found it soft. It was a chilling portent and one that came true a few hours later when Hannah passed away. Several years later, at a local seance where the medium used an Ouija board, the answers provided to questions came from a 'spirit' with an intimate knowledge of the town and the family present. The 'spirit' voice answered to the name 'Polly,' the nickname given to Hannah as a girl! So disconcerting were the events of the evening and the spirit's revelations that those present resolved never to attend another seance. Hannah Pettinger was my grandmother, and I was present at the event.

As late as the 1940s, in the blackouts of the war, there were reports of residents from the Epworth Turbary seeing apparitions. One case, reported to the authorities, spoke of a 'dark shape' that crossed so realistically in front of the witness's bicycle that he applied his brakes in fear of running into the shadowy form. Some people even reported seeing a strange pinkish glow that kept appearing and vanishing in much the same way as a flashing beacon. It did elicit an investigation by the authorities, not because they wanted to prove or disprove the existence of some supernatural force, but rather to discount the possibility of the lights coming from an enemy spy!

Even by the fourth year of the war, when the tide o battle began to turn in favour of the Allies, the authorities remained vigilant to the threat of German subterfuge. Arthur Ellison of Epworth, working as a relief post van driver, had taken heed of the instruction given to drivers to not stop for any reason in between delivery and pickup points as there had been a spate of holdups. Arthur was a careful and considerate driver and, having been a member of the Automobile Association since the early 1920s, saw himself as something of 'a knight of the road.' He was returning from his round one night as twilight drifted into darkness and as he drove past Misterton Cemetery he caught sight of a figure in the subdued headlights. The figure moved swiftly from the left and stood in his path, waving its arms frantically in front of its face. Immediately Arthur faced a dilemma; his instincts told him to pull over and assist, but his instructions were clear – do not stop for any reason. In the split second it took to make up his mind, Arthur pushed his foot down on the accelerator, thinking, when the figure realised he was not going to stop, it would move out of the way. No such thing happened, and Arthur admitted closing his eyes as if to blank out the shock of the expected collision. After travelling on for several yards, Arthur realised that the crash, for which he had braced himself, had not happened. Glancing in his rearview mirror, trying to discern the darkness of the road from the gloom of the shaded surroundings, Arthur saw nothing! Overcoming a desire to make sure he had not severely injured someone, he drove on.

When he reported the experience at the depot, the first thing his supervisor did was check the front of the van; he found no marks or dints to suggest there may have been a collision. Even so, the two decided to take an unmarked vehicle back to the scene of the 'accident' and examine the ground. Carrying flashlights, they searched the area but could find no evidence of anyone suffering injury from a vehicle strike. The Post Office advised Arthur not to speak about the incident for fear of alarming the populace. A level-headed and judicious man, he kept it a secret into later life but always retained a belief that, on a February night in 1944, he had driven his van at a ghost.

In Crowle, there is a well-documented story that tells of a farmer meeting a mysterious person who said he could finish the construction of a road being built out from the town as long as the farmer promised not to watch. The farmer agreed, but curiosity overcame him and, when he heard tinkering and hammering, he sneaked back, hid behind a hedge and watched. To his surprise, he saw hordes of small men at work on the surface of the road. Inadvertently revealing his presence the men vanished before his eyes and the man who agreed the deal cursed him and the road, swearing it would forever remain unfinished.

*The Regal Cinema - Crowle, in its heyday
Photograph courtesy of Lee Spivey.*

Also in Crowle, a large stone found in a farmyard, and known to many as 'the black stone,' seemed to have 'unusual' powers. Again, as with many large stones in the Axholme area legend had it that, if someone moved the stone bad things would happen. In this case, it was the farmer's cattle that would die within the following year. It seems that on one occasion someone did remove the stone and, true to the narrative, not only did all the farmer's cattle die but he suffered a significant financial loss. It was only then that the stone reappeared mysteriously.*

Perhaps the highest profile of the ghost stories from Crowle are those associated with the Regal Cinema. Built on the site of a blacksmith's shop, by A. Kelsey and Son for Joseph Spivey, it seems a spirit the locals called 'Talky' Bill roamed the building accounting for muffled mumblings (hence the name 'Talky') and, at times, quite stentorian footsteps. When the cinema closed to reopen as a shop those who worked there were baffled one morning to find that overnight packets and tins had been 'moved' along shelves or

* *From 'Household Tales and Other Traditional Remains, collected in the Counties of York, Lincoln, Derby and Nottingham by Sidney Oldall Addy M.A.*

stacked elsewhere. One assistant, who had a penchant for Ribena, would often find bottles of the fruit drink lined up on her counter. The episodes were treated with humour until a new owner insisted on redesigning the layout of the shop. To minimise disruption, the owner asked the men undertaking the renovation if they would work throughout the night and agree to be locked in. They saw no problem with this, but the next morning when the staff came to open the shop, they found the men sitting with their backs to the wall and their knees drawn up under their chins. They told the owner they would not be working at the premises any more as through the night their tools had continually 'gone missing' only to appear again in some other part of the building. The possibility of one of the men playing practical jokes on his workmates remains a possibility, but to a man, they all declared they would not come back another night, and they were true to their word!

There are astrological links to the Isle also suggesting a lost zodiac, known only by an old saying, 'the Scorpio in Crowle,' meaning a time of ill omen. This reference occurs in the 'Manuscript in the Red Box' when Mr. Butharwick advises Frank Vavasour not to visit Crowle as his horoscope is in Mars and 'the town is ruled by Scorpio.' He goes on to say, 'Crowle is always unlucky for you.' 'Truly,' replies Vavasour. 'my horse once fell there, and once I came to disgrace for snoring under a sermon by Uncle Graves.' After some further discussion the pair decide to travel to Crowle but not until Vavasour 'had put on [his] topaz ring, and engaged to use prayer appointed for Times of War and Tumult.'

In August 1792, the son of a respectable farmer from Haxey undertook what to many was a trifling wager. He agreed to eat three dozen penny pies and drink a quart of ale, all within half an hour. When the time came to undertake the wager, a sizable crowd gathered to witness the event. The swarthy youth, 'long in the leg but of a swarthy girth' stepped up to the challenge, and although having already eaten a hearty tea, he swallowed 37 pies and downed the liquid in the allotted time. Having collected his winnings, he declared to those assembled that he would not be staying longer as he was due back home for his supper!

Some even claim the Isle as the template for the mythical 'Isle of Avalon' from the time of King Arthur. It is at best a tenuous assertion. As with other places that claim 'Avalon' as their own, there is little, if any, evidence that Avalon existed as a real place. Perhaps it was never perceived as an island existing in this world and may have been little more than a Celtic myth relating to a different world entirely.

A copse of trees on the road from Epworth to High Melwood where, in the 1950s and 60s locals reported seeing the form of a headless monk crossing the road as the car headlights lifted towards the summit.

CHAPTER SIX

Riot

MAYHEM

When, in 1626, King Charles and Cornelius Vermuyden reached an agreement to drain the levels of Hatfield Chase and Axholme, Francis Thornhill, a minor gentleman from Misterton, who had oversight of the copy orders pertaining to the Isle, became concerned. As far as he could ascertain the tenants of the manor of Epworth had a rightful claim to the land through the deed of their fourteen-century lord, John de Mowbray. This far reaching and, for its time unique document, barred de Mowbray's successors from making changes to the locals' rights of free access to all land on the manor. Acting upon Thornhill's opinion, the residents of Axholme used it as their reason to resist Vermuyden's scheme, resorting to civil disorder to achieve their aims. Surprisingly, and in something of a 'volte face,' in 1628 Thornhill wrote to Vermuyden to tell him that some three hundred 'rioters' (most of them women and boys) had broken the new bank over the River Idle, breaking planks and barrows in the process. He seemed concerned that these 'base' people might escape punishment. As for the 'baser Islonians,' they were well prepared to accept any punishment that might come their way. Aware that King Charles had personally instigated the scheme in league with Vermuyden their resentment of the pair knew no bounds. They even spoke openly of killing the king should he ever set foot on their land.

It was the Civil War, however, that provided the residents of Axholme with the means to elevate their quarrel and they were quick to profit from the confused situation. They saw it as their chance to rid the area of the Dutch settlers for good. With the execution of the King, and land under the control of Parliament there was no one to use royal prerogative to refuse their pleas through the courts. Led by Daniel Nodell, the fenmen's attorney, they petitioned the newly sovereign Parliament. Nodell spoke of the 'hearts of many thousand men, women and children, in the Isle of Axholme [who] have occasion to bless God for his deliverance, when they see that through your means the law of the land is become their protection in their estates, against usurpers and wrongdoers.' Unfortunately, hopes that Parliament would right their perceived wrongs came to nought and many an Islonian saw the sword and cudgel as their only means of protest. When a large crowd of Islonians gathered on Haxey Carr, Nodell stood at their head brandishing his sword. He claimed they were set on negotiating with those undertaking the drainage but it soon became clear they were not! Fifty of the assembled throng came on horseback; others carried clubs, sticks and forks – hardly the tools of negotiation and debate. Vermuyden and his men, not to be outdone, turned up to negotiate with three muskets, a flintlock, two pistols and various pitchforks and swords. There followed the most significant period of lawlessness ever seen in the area. Locals tore down the settler's houses, destroyed the corn in their fields and forced them to watch at gunpoint as the destruction took place. Increasingly ready to resort to violence, the one thing the locals lacked was some person of high profile to 'add weight' to their dispute. They found such a man in John Lilburne.

Revelling in his nickname of 'Freeborn John,' Lilburne was a leading advocate for the freedom of the 'common' people. He belonged to a group known as the Levellers (though he shunned the title himself). This group demanded regular elections, religious freedom, equality before the law, an end to conscription for war service, equal electoral districts according to population, and universal manhood suffrage. He was a man committed to overcoming oppression and injustice in all its forms and thrived on conflict for its own sake. His boorish style, coarse manners and emphasis on the natural rights of freeborn Englishmen, impressed the men of the Isle and they looked upon him as one of their own. Not averse to breaking heads or burning the houses of the hapless foreigners, Lilburne realised from the outset that, although rioting might harm the Commoners' cause, there were few other options. Having inflamed the locals with his rhetoric, he had to back up his oratory, so he and a group of Epworth men camouflaged themselves and set off to besiege the settlement at Sandtoft. Reports say Lilburne shouted, 'this is our common, you shall come here noe more unles ye be stronger than we.'

Locals break down sluice gates and destroy embankments. Detail taken from the Haxey Kneeler Tapestry.

Sometime later, over a period of ten days, he and his men destroyed eighty-two houses at Sandtoft as well as barns, stables and outhouses. The mob moved on to the church and, even though armed men guarded the doors, they broke in. Surprisingly, Lilburne prayed and preached in the church before the rioters buried animal carcasses under the communion table, ripped the Ten Commandments from the walls and stabled horses in the nave, causing untold damage. With some satisfaction, they used the area as common land with no regard for the graves of Participants. So confident of success was Lilburne that it is said he repaired a house at Sandtoft, which had been built for the minister and installed his servant there. True to his spirit, however, he continued to use the church as a stable and a cowhouse! For Lilburne, the incident and the preceding year had delivered just the outcome he thrived upon – pure theatre.

Over many decades of disturbance, there were no less than thirty-one pitched battles between the Commoners and the Participants. It was said that Nathaniel Reading, a barrister who was counsel for the Commoners but later switched sides, was involved in all of them. Supposedly, he lived to the age of one hundred years and seemingly spent fifty of those involved in the troubles on the Isle!

When several commoners entered land belonging to the Nantes' family, according to Sarah Nantes they 'took [our] beasts, all armed with clubs, staves, forks and spades and so continued until they had destroyed all.' They threatened to 'drown' the land again which would see the foreigners having to 'swim away like ducks.' When six rioters returned and 'did pull down all the houses,' one told her 'it was a shame the Parliament should give away their commons [for] they were a Parliament of clouts' – an incendiary comment for any Islonian to make for it challenged the authority and legitimacy of Parliament.

The original investors received little or no profit for changing sixty thousands acres of Axholme land from wetland to meadow. What became apparent, however, was the whole episode laid bare the corruption in government. The Privy Council had provided resources to put down the riots; the Exchequer condoned Vermuyden's attempts at blackmail, and commissioners neglected their responsibility for maintaining the banks that protected the low-lying areas from inundation. Even so, some chroniclers maintained that the Axholme peasantry claimed their rights under false pretences and were little more than greedy and ungrateful oafs! After all, the promise was that, although 'giving up' two-thirds of their rightful land, the increased profitability of the remaining third would more than compensate their loss. Reducing Vermuyden's drainage to pure economics, the Exchequer pointed to an increase in the value of the land from eight pence to thirteen shillings and to the fact that corn grew where once there had been just sedge and reed. Another 'guarantee' was an improvement in their health for, when the bog land returned to earth and mists no longer shrouded their lives, the debilitating effects of 'Marsh Fever' would be a thing of the past. All of this, however, and the actions of the Crown and its legislative processes, achieved little save cementing further the locals' loathing of authority.

A story, possibly apocryphal, but one that highlights their hatred of the settlers, tells of some locals tying a Dutchman to the branches of an uprooted elder tree and setting him adrift on the River Trent. Fastened about his neck was a sign on which they had written the words 'Go Back to Dutchland.' It seems the man survived the ordeal when the tree root snagged among the reeds on the east bank. Thankfully his rescuers did not share the Isle's hostility to 'foreigners' and treated him well before sending him on his way!

Throughout the drainage, Vermuyden's controversial personality saw him reluctant to negotiate and content to rely on royal support. Some saw him as a hero: an engineer from the Dutch Golden Age who brought civilisation to unappreciated, feeble-minded English peasants. To others he was the embodiment of evil: a man who made calamitous errors, ruined a rare ecosystem and deprived the poor of their long-held birthright to common land. Scholars still argue over the benefits of Vermuyden's work. Dugdale in his 'History of Imbanking and Draining,' published in 1662, deplored the opposition seeing the islanders as obstinate, ignorant peasantry clinging to a miserable life because they were incapable of grasping the superior benefits of drainage.' Joan Thirsk in her works on the 'Rural Economy of England' (1984) maintains that the charge of ignorance should be brought 'against Crown and Parliament, for they were utterly ignorant of conditions in Axholme before the drainage.' She concludes that Vermuyden's drainage did not create an agricultural economy where none existed but substituted an arable economy for a pastoral economy. Whatever the merits and demerits of the scheme, a land scarred by drains, dykes, catchwaters and sewers, is now the richest arable region in Lincolnshire.

Two hundred years later it was the women of Epworth who rioted. Led by Tommy Wrigglesworth a bricklayer of the town, these women risked transportation if caught and tried. Successive harvests on the Isle had been poor, and the women determined that somehow they had to feed their families. Entering the granary of Jacky Maw, a wealthy bachelor farmer, they each took a bushel of his 'good' corn. Each woman laid a sovereign on Jacky's desk to compensate him for the loss – it was, after all, not a theft borne out of poverty but out of need. Jacky declared he would never touch the money and it lay on his desk for many months until his family persuaded him to put the coins in a drawer. Having acceded to their request and true to his word, the drawer remained closed until his death!

The riot which would go on record as one of the most orderly ever to have taken place happened during a period of widespread agricultural unrest known as the Swing Riots. Agricultural workers rose in protest over land enclosure, low wages and the increasing threat of mechanisation and went 'abroad' maiming cows, breaking threshing machines and burning hayricks. The farmers of Axholme were little affected by these riots with only sporadic incendiary attacks taking place at West Butterwick.

Sir Montague Cholmeley.

In direct contrast, when parties of Liberals and Conservatives reached Epworth on the morning of 3 June 1852 to canvass for the forthcoming parliamentary election, they assembled to the north of the town on the aptly named, Cut Throat Hill. The Liberals, supporters of Sir Montague Cholmeley, eager to put on a 'grand show,' arranged for supporters from across Lincolnshire to travel by rail to Gainsborough, then by steamer to Owston Ferry, from where they walked in procession up to Epworth. Alerted to this the Conservatives, supporting their candidate Mr. Banks Stanhope, braced themselves for trouble; if any arose, they pledged to return like-for-like. Shortly before twelve o'clock, the two parties marched into the town waving their blue and pink banners. Arriving at the Market Place for what the newspapers described as a 'monster meeting,' they found everything in readiness for each group to address their supporters. To try to ensure a fair meeting, locals had erected a platform under the windows of the Red Lion, dividing the Liberal and Conservative sides of the podium with a rail. They expected a large crowd but were taken aback when almost four thousand began to fill the Market Place.

On the opposite side of the Market Place, in front of the Manor Court House, Captain Healey assembled a troop of about 150 Conservative supporting horsemen in a semi-circle two or three deep. He, too, expected trouble as he had warned several of his friends not to venture to the town as there was the likelihood of a 'battle' taking place. Although there was a long established Isle practice of electioneering from horseback, the custom in Epworth was for horsemen to dismount on Lancaster Lane and walk their horses into the Market Place. On this occasion, however, Healey's troop chose to remain in their saddles. The locals saw this action as an affront, and their mounted presence raised the already simmering tension. Between the horsemen and the platform was enough space for the public to gather and listen but some Epworth folk turned their backs to the platform and began to shout abuse at Healey for flouting established practice.

The supporters on the Conservative side of the Market Place, were in position first, and some spilt into the space allocated to the Liberals. As the Liberals entered the Market Place, they assembled their band on the side of the hustings allotted to them; the rest moved into position between the band and the mounted horsemen. To create more space, they began to elbow the Conservatives across the Market Place. As the Leeds Mercury reported, 'nothing could exceed the disgraceful conduct of the men who wore Sir Montague Cholmeley's party colour.' Waving their banners, they caused the horses to panic, and some animals began to back away. Sir Robert Sheffield, the Conservative speaker assigned to open the meeting, could not be heard as the horsemen responded to the threat by using their riding-whips to push back against the Liberals. Some reports contend that the riders had filled these with lead to create greater injury when striking down at those who stood in their way. While the Liberals demanded the cavalry remove their horses, the Conservatives demanded silence so they could hear Sheffield's speech. Captain Healey dismounted and tried to reason with the Liberals, but the situation had become irretrievable. At some point in the proceedings, the Conservatives unfurled a black flag, a demand under the 'rules' of piracy they would accept surrender or death. This action saw the Liberals turn their flags around and use the stems as staves; some even dragged branches from nearby trees to use against the riders, brandishing them as though 'wild Indians.' Under such provocation, the horsemen closed formation and charged the Liberals out of the Market Place and up to the King's Head Hotel where they sought refuge. Sir Robert Sheffield took the opportunity to finish his address but, just as the band began playing 'Oh dear what can the matter be,' the Liberals returned, greatly strengthened by ruffians in butchers' aprons. Armed with broken flagstaffs and knotty clubs 'as thick as men's arms,' they moved forward in unison and began chanting: 'Take your horses away.'

As both sides engaged in a pell-mell 'battle,' sticks, stones and ginger beer bottles flew through the air 'and blood streamed down may a brow and cheek.' Several of the crowd took their anger out on the horses striking indiscriminately at their heads, eyes, mouth, neck and legs. One horse had its eye 'dashed out' by a particularly savage blow. Two or three ruffians aimed blows at Captain Healey with their flagstaffs as he rode through the crowd waving his hat in a futile attempt to restore order. As the speakers on the platform scrambled to safety through the open windows of the Red Lion, it gave way and crashed to the ground. Some members of the crowd picked up the broken fragments to increase the potency of their weapons while others took to throwing stones, 'more than half the size of a man's head' at the upstairs windows of the inn in a vain attempt to provoke a reaction from those inside. Eventually, however, the crowd drifted away, and by three o'clock a semblance of law and order returned to the Market Place. That night, about a hundred supporters from the Conservative ranks attended a 'splendid dinner in the Red Lion Inn which was very tastefully and appropriately decorated for the occasion.'

It transpired later that, on the day of the meeting, both sides had come intent on using it not to convince their supporters or opponents by reasoned argument but to put on a 'show of strength.' They had brought along some hooligans (mainly navvies), and several of these were drunk. Many held the Liberals responsible for starting the riot arguing that had they not attempted to dominate the hustings then probably the event would have passed off peacefully. At first, the authorities believed a man from Belton had died in the skirmish, but the story proved to be false. John Maw of Epworth was the only severely injured casualty having fallen beneath the hooves of the restless horses. Some publications, taking up Captain Healey's warning, described the incident as the 'Battle of Epworth.' The Hull Packet went further and labelled it as 'one of the most extraordinary riots in the annals of English electioneering.' Outrageous though the reports were, it appears likely that having occurred in a small rural community it achieved greater notoriety and received more press coverage than similar disturbances in the major towns of the time. 'I declare most distinctly,' Healey went on to say, 'I was not at all aware such an emblem existed until I drove into town with Mr. Stanhope on the morning of the meeting, and that even to this day I know not with whom it did originate.'

The incident brought stinging rebukes and denials from both parties present. Captain Healey stated 'that the black flag exhibited at our late Protectionist Meeting at Epworth' did not originate from him. Cholmley wrote in the Stamford Mercury that the charge of bringing 'hired men from Gainsborough was a monstrous falsehood.' Banks Stanhope, also writing in the Stamford Mercury, positively denied that 'horsemen carried loaded bludgeons on that day.' His summation went on to suggest that Sir Montague 'put no trust in the good faith of the Isle men. Had he not brought friends from a distance; had the blue band, backed by the bludgeon men, not attempted to obtain possession of the front of the hustings; had they not been cheered on by some who, from their position in society, ought to have set a better example, it is clear that the riot would not have happened.'

The riot at Epworth did not go unnoticed however, and led to the government introducing legislation to curtail expenditure on bands, flags and paid helpers. The Liberals saw support for their candidate, Sir Montague Cholmeley, not a popular figure among Protestant Wesleyans plummet to 24%, the lowest for any part of North Lincolnshire and this in no small measure led to him losing the election. One of those saved from injury by being dragged through a broken sash window, however, Cholmeley would return to Epworth five years later in less troublesome times. He would dine with friends at the King's Head along with two-hundred freeholders from the Isle who turned out to support him! It seems the electors of Axholme forgave his involvement in the riot as the reason for the celebration was his re-election to Parliament in the general election of 1857.

CHAPTER SEVEN

Home Medicine, Quackery and Alchemy

MISADVENTURE

One has only to flick through John Wesley's Primitive Physic published in 1747 to get an idea of the sort of cures promoted in the eighteenth century. It would be wrong to place his attempts to improve the health of those with whom he had the most contact by labelling them as some have done as 'quackery.' Wesley's primary ambition for Primitive Physic was to provide: 'a plain and easy way of curing most diseases, to set down cheap, safe, and easy medicines, easy to be known, easy to be procured, and easy to be applied by plain and unlettered men.' Contemporary surgeons and apothecaries ridiculed the book for being reliant on cures based in folklore and founded in ignorance.

Those who took a more Puritanical approach believed the role of a preacher to be that of a spiritual adviser and not a deliverer of medical advice. They argued that medical problems were God's way of alerting the sufferer to a spiritual need. Once acknowledged, the power of the spirit would lead to physical renewal.

Wesley, by contrast, was open to the notion that in cases of physical ailment it was always God's intent to heal. The remedies and cures are not his (although he does indicate those that he believes to be the most effective), but the way the book is laid out is his idea. There are many remedies in the book that reference sensible and practical solutions to help cure illness and disease. Others, however, have little or no basis in medical fact and where these proved successful can be put down to coincidence; the sufferer having recovered irrespective of the supposed cure. Wesley sought

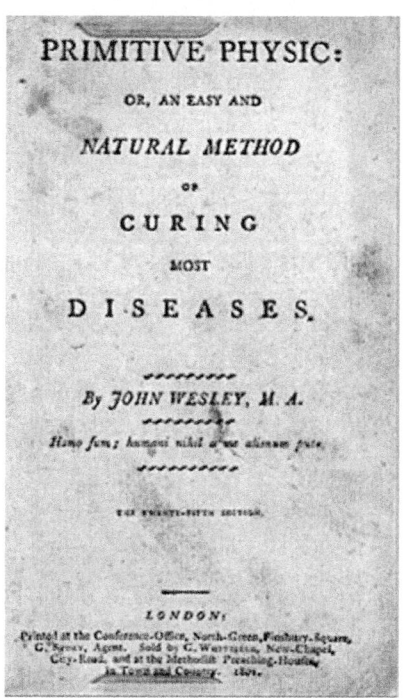

Original frontispiece from Wesley's 'Primitive Physic'.

no financial gain being neither the producer nor the peddler of such remedies. His journeys around the country no doubt brought him into contact with many who declared this or that to be an infallible remedy. He even encouraged his preachers to carry copies of the book, recommend it and, where appropriate, enhance it with their ideas. His aim, in his own words, was simple; to provide a 'plain and easy way of curing most diseases, to set down cheap, safe, and easy medicines, easy to be known, easy to be procured, and easy to be applied by plain and unlettered men.' Wesley goes on to say, 'I have purposely set down several remedies for each disorder; not only because all are not equally easy to be procured at all times, and in all places: but likewise because the medicine which cures one man, will not always cure another of the same distemper.'

Primitive Physic is widely believed to have been the most popular medical book of its day, running to twenty-three editions.

That said, many of the guileless and unsophisticated residents of the Isle happily took 'little better than useless' cures. For countless years, the outlandish claims and charisma of the hucksters brought Isle folk into the market places of Axholme's towns and villages. On feast days and market days, their calls would echo down the streets bringing the credulous to witness some 'miracle cure' that often involved paid locals declaring themselves restored to health.

A hundred years later, when Mary Groise of Owston Ferry developed an abscess on her back she resorted to one of the many Victorian cure-all medicines available to the public - in her case, Clarke's World-famed Blood Mixture. This 'great blood purifier and restorer for cleansing and clearing the blood from all impurities' came highly recommended. The creators claimed it would cure old and ulcerated sores on the neck, cancerous ulcers, glandular swellings, sore legs, scrofula, scurvy, remove blackheads and pimples on the face, and clear the blood of all impure matter. The concoction was pleasant to taste and supposedly 'free from anything injurious to the most delicate constitution of either sex.' It seems Mary found it much to her liking as she drank thirteen bottles of the stuff in quick succession and declared herself cured.

Like a multitude of other cure-alls, when the British Medical Association analysed the product they found it to be mainly water, with a little sugar, potassium iodide and traces of alcohol, chloroform and ammonia. The cost to produce a standard bottle of the mixture came to one old penny, but Clarke's sold the product for two shillings! The mixture continued to thrive under the business Mr. Clarke set up, the Lincoln and Midland Counties Drug Company. Although the formula changed over the years – including the addition of sarsaparilla – it remained on the market until the 1960s.

Around the turn of the twentieth century, many persuasive advertisements appeared in the Crowle Advertiser and the Epworth Bells. Local chemists broadcast their own remedies as well as being agents for more worldly cures such as Reverend Joseph's Universally Acclaimed Prescription for 'maladies including, loss of energy, melancholy, premature decay, loss of manhood, exhausted vitality, youthful imprudence, dimness of sight, brain fag, blotches and every form of disease peculiar to the Urinary Organs.' The Reverend G. Lee, late primitive Methodist Minister of Crowle, wrote commending a well-known blood purifier. His commendation stated, 'after suffering severely from ulcers and boils for several weeks which incapacitated me from my regular duties, I took a single bottle of your mixture and all appearance of skin disease promptly and permanently disappeared.'

Bells, chemists of Epworth, Whiteheads of Owston Ferry and Farnsworths of Haxey stocked Berry's Diamond Ointment and claimed it healed Scurvy, Ringworm and bad legs, and was especially valuable for reducing the swelling and itch of piles! Understandably, the fact that it contained significant levels of mercury did not make the advertisement. Similarly, Axe's store in Belton sold Adcos Ointment, guaranteed to eradicate Eczema, chilblains, bruises and sores being and was free from 'poisonous colourings.' Archers in Epworth sold 'the most palatable and richest cod liver oil' and, for those unable to tolerate this, they suggested a milder form of petroleum oil (a liquid hydrocarbon which when used internally suppressed the body's ability to break down fats). Another offering was 'pectoral emulsions' that much suited 'frail, languid or delicate girls and women, giving them strengthened blood.' This concoction included almond oil, egg yolk, cinnamon water, mucilage (a sticky extract from plant fibres), Ipecacuanha Wine (which in small doses did stimulate the appetite but in larger ones brought on bouts of severe vomiting) and syrup of tolu (a sap-like resin used to treat dry skin).

The Epworth Bells published their own 'cure for rheumatism, kidney trouble and bladder troubles.' Stating that they knew the readers of the paper appreciated good advice, they were glad to be able to publish the following advice from a prominent physician who declared: 'It is astonishing to know the prevalence of kidney trouble and other diseases, such as rheumatism, bladder and liver troubles, which are almost invariably caused by weak kidneys. It is said on good authority that fully one-third of the people of the United Kingdom who have reached the age of maturity are more or less afflicted with kidney trouble in some form. The most dangerous feature of this disease is the fact that many people have it without their knowledge, and consequently neglect it until it has reached a dangerous stage.' The recipe the Bells advocated contained; 1oz gentian tincture, 1oz syrup of rhubarb, 1oz liquid bar kola compound and 5oz syrup of ginger. The Bells' suggestion was for 'a teaspoon to be taken after each meal and at bedtime.'

There can be few who lived in the 1950s who do not remember being treated with liquid paraffin, castor oil or syrup of figs to aid digestion and keep bodily functions regular. Sore throats might be 'dressed' with a Kaolin poultice; a clayey paste heated to boiling point, spread on a bandage then applied under the chin – so hot that on occasions it left the skin burnt and blotchy. Those unable to afford the commercial product simply trawled the river mud from the banks of the Trent. It was cheap, readily available and apparently just as effective!

Those who have read John Hamilton's book 'Captain John Lister' will note how he blends historical fact with a novelist's license in his story of the Isle.* Early in the book, he points the reader to the sympathetic character of the titular hero as he watches a melancholy procession of women and diseased and deformed children, troop toward Burnham on the morning of Haxey Feast. Passing before him Lister watches an 'intermittent stream of wayfarers. Nearly all the children seemed to be afflicted with deformity or disease. Faces disfigured by sores and blotches,

Burnham Well. Photograph by Jonathan Thacker and licensed under CC Licence.

eyes inflamed or blinking, or blind, crooked backs and crippled limbs, forms shrunk and shrivelled, passed by in a monotonous procession of distortion and suffering.' To Lister, it appears as a vision of Hell and when he questions a local innkeeper over the trail of sick people, the man tells him: 'They are going to the Holy Well at Nether Burnham. 'Tis a famous spring, and has been many ages, and on this day there is virtue in the water to cure almost any disease or sickness in a child if be dipped before noon.' To add greater emphasis to the story, Hamilton has the innkeeper telling Lister that infected folk come from as far away as Nottinghamshire and Yorkshire.

Determining to see the spectacle for himself Lister follows the path leading to the well. The route takes him past haggling hucksters, quack doctors, buxom damsels busy filling pots and horns with foaming ale, and dealers in cheap merchandise all eager to sell their wares to the gullible and the naive. One of the sellers along the way was Mrs. Linacre, an enterprising lady of Dutch descent. She

* *Captain John Lister written by John Hamilton. The story tells of Lister's escapades as he attempts to keep order among the marshmen and foreign settlers of Axholme.*

made it her occupation, every summer's day to serve mineral water from the spring. Reputedly, the water's properties cured sterility in married women, so long as 'folk partook of the waters before noon.' Those who drank the water spoke of its particular virtues and of receiving great benefit from its curative powers. Arriving at her little shed by the spring, Mrs Linacre would take out her glasses and rinse them out before the travellers passed. She would sit in her hut when it rained and under a tree when it was fine. Her smile cheered those who were sick and pleased those who simply paused at her stall out of base curiosity.

Supposedly the site where King Oswald met his death in battle, Burnham Well was also known as the 'Well of the Blessed Redeemer.' Revered over by myriad generations, the well's popularity waned by the early nineteenth-century and the area fell into disrepair. In his book on the History of the Isle, Stonehouse notes: 'about one hundred and twenty years ago, the concourse of visitors was so great that a Village Feast was held at the same time and at a much later period conveniences were annually made for the use of the bathers, and gingerbread-stalls and other slight reflections were provided on the spot. This practice has, however, of late years fallen altogether into disuse. The spring now appears in a dirty and neglected state.' Later, and in one of its earliest editions, the Epworth Bells took up the call for reinstating the well, 'firmly believing in the efficacy of the Burnham water in the cure of some outward bodily complaints,' and of the 'desirability of the public availing themselves of the water.'

Canon L. D. Ravins, Vicar of Owston Ferry in the 1960s, held the opinion that the water may well have medicinal qualities as an unmistakably sulphurous smell seemed to come from the area. Analysis of the water did not reveal any sulphur, but it did show the presence of Magnesium and Calcium Sulphates and Calcium Bicarbonate, all elements found in spa waters. Taking a cue from

Stonehouse, however, many contended that it was the frigidity of the cold water that dulled the complaint rather than any magical, restorative power.

In 1817, a young man from Keadby, who had been in a poor state of health for quite some time spoke to Mathias Pepper, a farrier of Crowle, about his problems. No matter what he tried nothing relieved the pain he felt in his lower abdomen. Pepper diagnosed trapped wind and advised him to drink a 'quantity' of rate water, a putrid concoction of rotting flax stems steeped in a peaty liquid. The young man took Pepper's advice and after a time passed a tapeworm some eight and a half feet in length. His condition improved rapidly!

In 1403, Henry IV banned the practice of 'multiplying' base metals into noble ones. From then on, anyone found practising alchemy could face imprisonment and in the most severe cases, death. This threat did not deter John Lound, vicar of Haxey, who in 1414 found himself accused of attempting to change iron into gold and silver. He did not deny the charge but sought to justify his actions by claiming he was following a similar process to that used by Jesus when turning water into wine at the wedding in Cana. He argued further that, as a vicar, his congregation held strongly the belief that they were partaking of the body and blood of Jesus when celebrating communion. As a final defence, Lound asserted that true to his faith his engagement with alchemy was a means of relating it to the spiritual conversion of the human soul. Quite literally, he was raising a 'golden' human from a base of latent evil. The above arguments were used by many who practised the 'art' of alchemy but, in Lound's case, it did little to sway the authorities. Sent to gaol in Spital-in-the-Street, he then transferred to the prison in Lincoln. It must have been deemed punishment enough as soon after he was bailed but it brought to an end his tenure at Haxey after just one year.

CHAPTER EIGHT

Death on the Tracks

MISADVENTURE

The Axholme Joint Railway (AJR) was lauded as an engineering enterprise akin to the magnitude of the drainage scheme some 250 years previously. The project, first mooted in 1833, took over seventy years to come to fruition. When complete, the hope was of a communication network that would bring significant change to the lives of Axholme residents. To this end, the line was seen as a vital link to the main lines to Doncaster and beyond, and hopes were high that the railway would bring prosperity and reduce isolation. To celebrate the cutting of the first sod, banners, flags and arches festooned the towns and villages, with slogans such as: 'After fifty years suspense ended – patience rewarded,' 'Progress and Prosperity' and ' Success to Agriculture.'

The inaugural run from Goole to Crowle took place in August 1903, but it was on Monday 2 January 1905, that thousands turned out to witness the Official Opening of the whole line. It was a day the Epworth Bells called 'The Dawn of a New Era.' As the train entered Epworth station from Belton with eighty-one people already on board, the reporter spoke of 'hearty cheers' filling the air. None cheered louder than Mr. W. A. Ross of Belton who celebrated his good fortune at being the first person to buy a ticket. The train took almost an hour to make the journey from Haxey Junction to Goole, but the general opinion was that the trucks and carriages ran smoothly with a minimum of friction. However, some complained that entering and alighting carriages proved tricky as the steps were not sufficiently close enough to the platform.

Although viewed by many as a force for good, the line was not without controversy, particularly during its construction. In late 1902, fifteen-year-old William Woodhead from Burnham, working as a point's turner near the cutting at Epworth, was coupling a wagon as the train approached at three miles an hour. The coupling chain was a temporary arrangement as the original one was under repair. This adjustment was not as secure as the original but deemed sufficient for the process. As William moved the striking rod into place, he became entangled in the point's lever. The action pitched him towards the track and into the path of the advancing train. Although a fireman managed to pull William out of the way, he stumbled back onto the line. The engine and a carriage went over his foot near the ankle smashing it badly. Although the newspaper report records no other injuries, William's must have been more severe as he died 'from shock to the system' eight hours after arriving at Doncaster Infirmary. At the inquest, the jury returned a verdict of 'accidental death' adding, 'we think there is negligence on the part of some unknown person, but the company's to blame.'

In another fatal accident in the same year, William King of Belton was with a gang of seven men riding a trolley down an incline at about six miles an hour. Without warning, one of the wheels on the trolley broke free. As the appliance derailed, the men jumped clear but as William attempted to leap from the trolley he caught his clothes on a brake handle, and this pitched him forward head first onto a sleeper. Some of his co-workers took William home unconscious but he died before medical help arrived.

Just before Christmas 1903, George Brock, a twenty-three-year-old labourer, at work excavating the cutting near Maw's Mill, struck a stone with his pickaxe. This action deflected his blow into a hole drilled to contain a live charge. He was heard to cry out in alarm just before the charge exploded. The force from the resulting blast blew George 20 yards across the line. Injuries from the blast and the subsequent fall left him in a 'dreadfully shattered condition.' Beyond all help, he was taken home dead! All work on the line stopped and the foreman instructed an investigation to begin immediately. This led to the shocking discovery of several other unexploded cartridges in holes nearby. At the inquest some weeks later, Charles Cordock, a chargeman on the construction, stated that he had filled several holes with gelignite on the day but none close to where the explosion occurred. The firing was done by an electric battery and as far as he knew there weren't any shots left unexploded. He went on to explain that if any hole failed to explode it was the custom to drill another within a foot of the original one; the explosion from this being sufficient to set off the one that did not explode. He recalled it being five or six weeks since he last charged any holes in the area where George's accident happened. During the past three years, the construction team used over twenty-three tons of gelignite on the line, and there had been no other 'rogue' explosions. When pressed, Cordock admitted that some gangers had occasionally charged holes themselves in a bid to speed up the work and some of these did so having had no formal training in the use of gelignite. At the inquest, the jury deliberated for half an hour before returning a verdict of 'accidental death' with a simple recommendation that greater care should be taken in future when laying charges. The coroner stated that the Local Government Board had been invited to be present at the inquest but, 'as these accidents were so common they did not think it necessary to attend.'

Over the years following, several other railway workers would meet their death on the railway, and at least two troubled souls would use the tracks to commit suicide. However, accidents on the AJR were not the first to claim the lives of Axholme residents and rail workers. Before its construction, three other lines crossed the Axholme area. To the north ran the Hull and Doncaster branch line; in the south, the Doncaster to Lincoln line and almost cutting the Isle in half, the line from Grimsby to Doncaster.

As early as 1867 there were reports of fatalities at Crowle Station. Thomas Graham, a twenty-two-year-old guard, assisting in a shunting process, was knocked down and killed when the axle of a wagon broke. Some years later Robert Cotton a fifty-nine-year-old platelayer crossed the lines just as the engine driver started the engine. The appliance, which had been taking on water, knocked him down, fracturing his left thigh, crushing his foot and causing severe internal injuries. His workmates rushed to get him to Doncaster Infirmary, but doctors were unable to save his life.

A year later, in the early hours, local policeman P.C. Tuffs found a badly mutilated man jammed between the metals of the track. He appeared to have been run over by a train, one of the wheels passing over part of his head, severing the scalp and smashing his jaw. Despite this and having one of his feet completely separated from the leg, the man showed signs of life, so Tuffs wired for help. A trolley arrived and conveyed the man to Crowle Station where Dr. Renton waited. Station staff confirmed the man as Ben Sykes of Crowle Wharf, and it was here he was taken. Dr. Renton along with Dr. Hall from Althorpe attended to Ben's injuries and decided to amputate the injured leg. Ben remained in a critical condition for some time but eventually recovered sufficiently to lead a reasonably active life.

Another avoidable accident happened soon after to a seventeen-year-old Crowle lad called Hind, working as an assistance lamp hand. His duties included crossing the line and standing in the six-foot gap between the two lines to deliver the signal. Young Hind arrived at his post in time to signal to the Doncaster to Grimsby train but failed to hear the train coming from the opposite direction. This train knocked him down cutting off one of his hands and severely injuring his head. Station workers disconnected the wagons from the train, and this then took him to Doncaster Infirmary. Here the house surgeon requested the stationmaster at Doncaster contact Crowle Station to summon the parents as he feared he would have to amputate the arm. The unfortunate boy had been at work for less than a week!

In an accident that was almost a sad parody of the previous one, another local man, John O'Sullivan, an electrical engineer from Keadby, fell into danger in the six foot. In April 1922 he was examining the bridge at 10.15 a.m. when he noticed a goods train approaching from Scunthorpe. Sensibly he stepped aside into the gap between the rails, but somehow the guards' van caught him on the shoulder and threw him onto the other line and into the path of the passenger train travelling from Doncaster. John's head hit one of the carriages and he fell in the six-foot. Severely injured, those present rushed him to Scunthorpe Hospital, but he was beyond all help.

The line to the south of the Isle that ran through Haxey Gate Station also saw its fair share of accidents. In 1882, Elizabeth Nightingale, described as a 'sensible and steady woman,' was accidentally run over by a train. Elizabeth was a fifty-five-year-old house manager who two months earlier had worked as a deputy at a large lodging-house in Hammersmith, London. Giving evidence at the inquest, held at the Great Northern Hotel, Thomas Corden, the train driver, stated that he was driving a passenger train and leaving Haxey Gate Station at 10.34 a.m. Approaching the crossing at Idle Bank at a speed of 40 miles an hour, and in driving rain, his fireman saw a woman stepping on to the crossing through the hand-gate. He opened the whistle and shouted 'Woman!' Corden looked out and, although seeing no one on his side, he shut off the steam and stopped the engine as quickly as he could without endangering the passengers. Leaving his mate in charge, he walked back down the line and came across Elizabeth's body ten yards to the side of the line. Returning to the engine, he noticed what appeared to be part of an apron hooked on the breakstay.

The jury heard evidence from the signalman, David Knight, who stated he had watched the approaching train but had not seen a woman on the crossing. Having weighed up the evidence, they returned a verdict of 'Accidental Death,' attaching no blame to anyone. It seemed clear, that Elizabeth despite being 'sound of hearing,' in her haste to cross the line had stepped onto the crossing unaware of the train's approach.

Isaac Charles Harris (known as Charles), son of the signalman at Haxey Gate Station, was a bright, energetic and highly independent twenty-month-old boy. On many occasions, his father allowed him into the signal box to 'help' direct the trains. In late 1895, around 5 p.m. as the day drew cold, his father sent Charles to their railway cottage home to get his hat. It appears Charles strayed close to the line and ended up a foot away from the rails. As the Gainsborough train passed, the draught from the engine drew him towards the tender, but it wasn't until the train stopped at Misterton, that the guard noticed blood on the steps and immediately instigated an investigation. Railway staff found Charles' body close to the station with his head completely smashed, his left arm severed off and his right arm and shoulder crushed to a pulp. The inquest delivered a verdict of 'Accidentally killed,' but recommended 'the company be requested to take some precaution for preventing children of tender years straying on the line at this station, and particularly that they will forthwith cause a closed paled fence to be erected round the cottages there.'

Within a few days of this tragedy, the Great Eastern (Harwich Boat) Express was speeding between Misterton and Haxey when the driver caught sight of movement on the line at Haxey Gate crossing. Immediately he blew the whistle and applied the brakes

EXPRESS IN PERIL.
BOAT TRAIN ACCIDENT near HAXEY.
Passengers Shaken.
ENGINE KILLS HORSE: MEN HAVE NARROW ESCAPE.

Headline from The Epworth Bells.

but the distance was not sufficient for the train to stop and it careered on, sparks flying from the locked wheels. Unaware of the unfolding drama, the passengers were jolted forward in their seats causing some of the less sanguine to scream and shout. As the train skidded toward the crossing, the driver noticed the gates had not been closed and saw a horse-drawn binder straddling the line. Mr. Charlesworth, in charge of the implement, seemed oblivious to the onrushing engine and it is possible the noise of the binder rattling across the tracks masked the sound of the oncoming train. It was left to the gatekeeper to assess the danger and running forward he began to urge on the horse-drawn contraption. Reacting to the danger, Mr. Charlesworth's made a frantic effort and succeeded in clearing the binder from the line. However, a carthorse attached by rope to the rear of the machine did not move fast enough and took the full force of the express train. The engine carried the poor animal forty yards down the line before the mutilated body slipped down the embankment. The engine also carried away a portion of the level crossing gate. The whole incident left everyone involved in a state of shock. The inquest found no plausible reason for the gates being left open, a decision that allowed Mr. Charlesworth to cross the line in front of an oncoming express.

When William Priest, foreman porter at Haxey Station looked across the station yard on the morning of 7 October 1899, he saw John Holland the youngest son of George Holland, delivering a cartload of potatoes. As John left the goods yard, leading the youngest horse by its rein, an express sped through the station. There had been no warning whistle as was the rule when there was no other train in the station, and the sudden sound of the approaching engine caused the horses to bolt. They headed towards the yard's exit, dragging John with them as he tried frantically to rein in the stampeding animals. As the horses reached the exit to the goods yard, the cart collided with a gate post, throwing John to the ground. Unable to roll clear quickly enough John took the full force of the cart as it passed over his thigh and turned him over. William Dawes, one of the team of porters, saw the incident and ran to John's assistance. He found him groaning but unable to speak. There was a mark on his clothing where the wheel passed over him and a thin streak of blood trickling from his nose, but there seemed to be no other injuries. Some other men working in the yard rushed to control the bolting horses as Walter Bawsor, assistant station master ran to help William Dawse. Together they carried John to the Railway Hotel and, helped by Nurse Alice Young who was staying at the hotel, they laid him on a sofa. Within minutes the doctor arrived, but by then it was clear John had little chance of surviving his ordeal – and so it proved, for within fifteen minutes of the doctor's arrival, John passed away. His father arrived a few minutes later.

At the inquest, his father told the coroner that, although young, John was experienced with the team of horses and had driven them alone on numerous occasions. One member of the jury said he had frequently heard the porters warn carters about approaching express trains. When the time came for the jury to deliver its verdict, it proved to be a straightforward case of 'accidental death,' though they did add the caveat, 'caused by losing control of his horses.' They attached no blame to those present in the yard, or to the driver of the express for not signalling its approach. They asked the coroner to pass on their condolences to John's family.

James Clynes and his wife Mary lived at the gatehouse on Field Road, Crowle. James was a platelayer but his job involved opening and closing the gates at the level crossing. He shared the role with his sixty-year-old wife Mary, who had helped him out for eight years. On Saturday 1 March 1922, after James had let the passenger train from Haxey through the gates, Mary returned from shopping around 7.30 p.m. This allowed James to go into town safe in the knowledge that Mary would be home to let the train through the gates on its return. There was a bell in the house to warn of approaching trains and an indicator to show which way the train was travelling. When a train arrived at Crowle from Belton, the accepted procedure was to open the gate to which the lamp was attached as it was the nearest to the house.

Somehow there must have been confusion in the system because as the train returned, Mary opened the 'wrong' gate first. The train was late and it is possible the indicator was out of order and still pointing towards Belton, the same way as when James let the train through earlier. James claimed he had informed his wife of this before leaving. As a result, in the darkness, the driver of the train failed to see the red light as it was turned away from his view. He assumed both gates were open and saw no reason to reduce speed. Mary must have been in the process of opening the second gate when the train hit her. Arthur Hindle, the fireman, felt the engine 'jar' and realised it had struck something other than the gates. Tom Balmforth, the driver stopped the train immediately and along with the guard, Mr. Chafor, left the cab to see what might have caused the obstruction. Using Chafor's lantern to light the way, they came upon Mary's body, lying on her back between the metals, seventeen yards north of the crossing. The engine's wheels had passed over her legs, severing both, and she had extensive injuries to her torso and head. Chafor's immediate response was to exclaim: 'Poor Mary, I'm afraid she's done!' Between them, they agreed that Balmforth would take the train on to Crowle and summon the doctor. The doctor arrived at the scene at 8.15 p.m. and found James Clynes stood over the body of his wife. The south gate of the crossing was open but the north gate 'had been smashed to pieces,' and broken timbers lay around the body.

At the inquest, the coroner placed no blame on the individuals at the centre of the tragedy but instructed the jury to consider the system in place at the time of the accident. The indicator was prone to error, the train was late and the system of 'ringing forward' did not register the receipt of a call so there was merely an assumption that the warning had been acted upon. The jury came to the conclusion that there should be red lamps fixed on both gates and the indicator system must be kept in good working order at all times. Despite the human and mechanical error, however, their verdict was 'death by misadventure.'

CHAPTER NINE

What's Your Poison?

MURDER

The nineteenth century was known as the arsenic century. Most households used this deadly chemical as a cheap cleaning material; the poor used it to control vermin; the fashion conscious used the powder to whiten the face and doctors prescribed it to treat the 'social evils' of syphilis. It was also the poison of choice for nineteenth-century murderers! Odourless, and tasteless when dissolved in water, it could easily be 'dispensed' to an unsuspecting victim. The twentieth most common element in the Earth's crust and a by-product of mining for metals such as copper, gold and zinc, arsenic was more readily available than ever during this period. It was extremely cheap and effective – it cost just one penny for half an ounce, enough to kill up to 50 people! Anybody, even a child, could go into almost any shop and buy enough poison to kill dozens of people. The majority of deaths related to arsenic, however, were unintentional, arising from incidental contact with this most infamous substance. Whether eaten, inhaled, absorbed through the skin by accident or administered intentionally this neurological toxin caused unimaginable suffering.

It was this powder that Poll Pilsworth, a familiar sight in Epworth, gave to some residents of the Epworth Poor House in 1790. To most in the town Poll came across as a kindly soul who used meagre ingredients to make simple delights for those living at subsistence level. Her signature dish was a spiced cake that she made from local crops and herbs collected from the wayside. Described by those who knew her as, 'a bonny stirring woman,' she worked as a cook at the Poor House. Every indication pointed to her doing her best to keep the children well fed and clean. Rumours began to circulate in the town, however, that Poll felt slighted in her desire for promotion to the post of mistress. Many believe it was this that led to an 'unfortunate incident' that cost the lives of three orphans and a family of tinkers.

Accounts from the time, tell of Poll poisoning the children by adding arsenic to her 'speciality' spiced cakes, served by the institution twice a week. The 'Leeds Intelligencer' reported that six-year-old Samuel Lunn, a poor boy placed in the Epworth Poor House only a few days earlier, spoke of feeling ill before suffering an agonising death. When others began vomiting violently, the manager sent for Dr. Ward. His immediate diagnosis was that they had been poisoned and he speculated this might have been in the cake eaten two days earlier. This theory gained further traction when a cockerel, given free run of the Poor House, died after seemingly ingesting poison in the crumbs thrown into the yard. A day later Jenny Storr, wife of Robert Storr, a short, thickset pedlar who travelled extensively throughout the neighbourhood selling spigots, faucets and small wooden spoons, died from convulsions.

Site of the Epworth Poor House on Queen Street.

Robert had already been taken ill on one of his rounds and claimed he 'felt like he had been poisoned' but, after completing his rounds, the feeling passed.

When Mr. Gervas the coroner arrived, he insisted on performing an autopsy on Jenny and little Samuel Lunn. In the boy's stomach he found nothing suspicious, but in Jenny's, there were traces of arsenic. At a hastily convened inquest the jury returned a verdict of accidental death for the boy, but in Jenny's case they concluded she must have been poisoned by a 'person or persons unknown.' Two days later Robert Storr's pains returned and he too died. As with his wife, small quantities of white arsenic showed up in his stomach. A young woman came forward claiming that a fortnight earlier Poll had persuaded her to go out and buy a pennyworth of arsenic. When the news broke in the town panic set in, many fearing they too might have been poisoned. Under questioning, Poll denied any involvement at first, but eventually, she confessed. A large crowd gathered at the Poor House bent on revenge. Seeing no way to escape, it seems Poll resorted to eating the remaining poisoned cakes and died 'in great agonies'. Some reports go so far as to suggest she was found with 'poison' in her pocket. At her inquest, held at the Poor House, the jury brought in a verdict of 'felo de se'(translated as a felon of themselves – in other words, suicide). *

Determined that Poll should not receive a compassionate burial, 'in a scene of great commotion,' a mob rushed into the building and seized Poll's body. They placed it in a rough coffin fixed to a plough-sledge and attached this to John Clayton's old horse. They then hauled the contraption over coarse ground to a crossroads in

* *The only recognised defence against 'felo de se' was adequate proof of a person's insanity. Unfortunately this was a state of mind that, at the time, was hard to determine and something to which few respectable families would care to admit. Mental illness was a poorly understood condition and the stigma attached often left those afflicted bereft of help and support.*

the town where Blow Row meets Burnham Road (known then as the 'guidepost'). As the coffin tumbled into a hastily dug grave, 'with a deliberate lack of finesse,' it broke open revealing Poll's face in a 'death stare.' At this point, someone stepped forward to drive two stakes through Poll's body to prevent her spirit walking. One witness remembers seeing the mell, a kind of huge mallet, being lifted high above the heads of the baying crowd before striking down. Witness records show, however, that not everyone present approved of the defiling of Poll's corpse for 'many shed tears on the occasion.' For some time, a large stone, about six yards north of the guidepost, marked her grave, but this later disappeared.

Over the years, many have claimed Poll was a misunderstood and persecuted individual and have sought to absolve her of the 'crime' believing her to be the victim of a cruel twist of fate rather than a cold-blooded killer who took delight in poisoning destitute individuals. Why, they ask, did Poll suddenly have a desire to become the mistress of the Poor House after so many years of hard work? How could this supposedly benevolent character suddenly take on the persona of a witch? Some have put forward the theory that the wheat used for the cakes was contaminated in some way. Perhaps, they argue, Poll did not kill herself through guilt but was also the victim of putrid wheat; wheat that even to this day causes problems for farmers. The Poor House had no well or pump, so water had to be carried by milk churn from a pond at Partner Closes. Could the poisonings have been the result of polluted water? There does, however, remain one intriguing and seemingly irrefutable fact. If the Leeds Intelligencer, a record from the time, reported the events correctly, the evidence given by the girl sent to buy arsenic, seals Poll's guilt. Or does it? Remember arsenic's many uses – there are some who cling to the hope that Poll may have requested the poison for a simple and humane reason – after all, the Poor House was infested with rats.

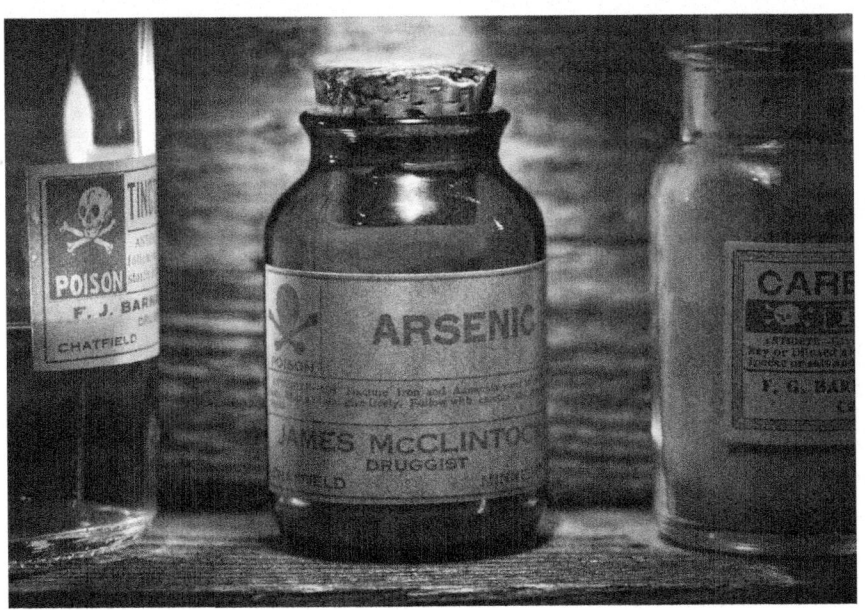

Arsenic - 'King of all poisons'.

Some months later the Stamford Mercury carried a report on an autopsy carried out on a Mary Pilsworth, described as 'a young woman in-service.' The report did not link this autopsy to the death of Poll but went on to state that two surgeons opened Mary's body and performed a 'strict examination' to ascertain her cause of death. It seems there had been stories circulating that her death was due to her having taken, or had administered to her, cantharides - an odourless and colourless poison taken from the secretions of the Blister Beetle. When crushed these soft-bodied beetles create a seemingly mystical concoction called Spanish Fly. The surgeons found no evidence of poison in Mary's body and directed the jury to bring in a verdict of 'death by natural causes.' It is an intriguing aside to the tale of Poll and a coincidence that both should have the same name. One is tempted to speculate that they may have been related!

Whatever the outcome, legend has it that Poll's restless spirit still wanders the area where her burial took place. Ironically, she lies close to Epworth Cemetery (constructed almost a hundred years after her death in 1881) along what was then called Gypsy Lane (later renamed Cemetery Lane). Those living in this area and previously unaware of the notorious events have reported mysterious sounds, resembling running footsteps and sobbing cries. It seems that, despite the efforts to quell her spirit, Poll still has unfinished business and is not yet ready to rest!

In a report in the July 1908 edition of the Stamford Mercury, George William Brown an ostler from Crowle surrendered to his bail on a charge of attempting to poison himself. He readily admitted to the offence and declared himself 'exceedingly sorry' as he now had work to go to after being dismissed from his post at a local hotel. Having taken this rejection of his abilities to heart he swallowed a dose of laudanum in an unsuccessful attempt to commit suicide. George had been drinking heavily before taking the poison and it seems the alcohol in his bloodstream, nullified the effect. The chairman remarked on the paradox of this case; it was the effects of the drink that saved the man's life and it was somewhat incongruous that he had to bind William over to the sum of £10 pending sentence.

It was not just the poisoning of humans that alarmed and sickened the locals. In Crowle in October 1857, a spate of dog poisoning rocked the town. One very valuable dog belonging to Mr. W.F. Cocking suffered a particularly agonising death, convulsing and foaming at the mouth before succumbing to the poison. The police made several enquiries and in one instance traced the footprints of one of the poisoned dogs to a hedge on which they found a piece of poisoned flesh. The Lincolnshire Chronicle questioned: 'What gratification there can be in the poisoning of a poor innocent dog we cannot tell, but one thing is certain, that the person or persons who are guilty of such an act richly deserve all that the law allows, and it is to be hoped that they will be detected and an example made of them.' The poisoning stopped abruptly soon after and it appears the authorities never identified the culprit(s).

CHAPTER TEN

Temporary Insanity

MISADVENTURE

Long regarded as a sin in Christian Britain, the period spanning the years of the late nineteenth to the early twentieth century, saw an unprecedented number of suicides occur in the Isle. Local newspapers from the time point to a suicide rate of 30 per 1000 head of population; a startlingly high proportion and the highest of any recorded in British history. 'Felo de se' remained illegal during this period, but the emphasis shifted from an act regarded as sinful to one of temporary insanity. Some academics put the rise in suicides down to the Victorians' morbid fascination with mental decay, madness and death. It was the height of the Gothic horror novel and books such as Dracula, The Phantom of the Opera and The Strange Case of Dr. Jeckyll and Mr. Hyde brought madness and terror to the lap of many a gullible reader. Somewhat of a dichotomy, just as the Victorian world began to reveal earth's mysteries, many sought understanding and meaning in books that questioned the ethics of the time and elevated the deranged antics of the central character to that of hero.

Human frailties that might lead a person to commit suicide are a sensitive and profound subject, but no study of the Isle's history can overlook the effect this had on those committing the act, or on those who bore its consequences. The fear of a shaming community meant, for many families, the best hope was to cover up the details of their loved one's death. It was often left to the compassionate nature of the coroner to suppress evidence of suicide and return a verdict of 'death by misadventure' instead.

In the period between 1864 and 1913, there were at least twenty-five suicides or attempted suicides reported across Axholme. The first involved John Voase, the landlord of the Darby and Joan Inn, at Crowle. On the day of his death, John seemed his usual self, going about his early morning chores in a businesslike manner. He collected his servants together, gave them their orders for the day and with them set about tidying up the pub from the previous evening. Later, as always, he went out to the stables to check on the horses. When he did not return, members of staff questioned his absence and some set off to search for him. They found him lying in the stables, propped up against a manger with his throat cut and a bloodied razor nearby. A quick check of the body found no sign of life. The Beverley and East Riding Recorder described the incident as 'shocking' and formulated the opinion that the deceased had been in 'a depressed state' for quite some time because of his ailing business.

In 1870, the wife of William Cooper of Haxey left him to tend to their pigs on the farm while she went to visit a neighbour. William had suffered a stroke six months earlier that left him partially paralysed, and his failing health had brought on a fear of being left alone. His wife knew this and believing him to be occupied for a period of time told him she would not be long. Upon her return, some thirty minutes later, she could not find William in the house or at the pig sty. Fearing he might have wandered off, she set off to search for him. Out in the yard she found the barn door bolted from the inside and began to suspect the worst. Unable to gain access, she went to her neighbour, George Lee, and together they returned to the barn. George saw a way into the barn and climbing onto the roof he gained access via some loose tiles. It took him some time but as he lowered himself to the floor, he saw William hanging from the rafters. He appeared to George to be 'quite dead.' Unable to cut William down on his own, George knew he had to open the barn door to seek help but this meant exposing William's wife to the horrific sight. Seeing her husband in such a state, the poor woman became most distraught but insisted on being the one to hold William's legs while George removed the rope from around his neck!

After stealing potatoes and some sacks belonging to John Taylor, forty-four-year-old Thomas Ramsey from Crowle found himself in custody at Crowle Police Station. Next morning he was up before the local magistrate, Rev. White, and it was he who remanded Thomas to appear before the Petty Sessions in Epworth. Thomas' father applied to have him released on bail pending trial, but Rev. White refused the request. On Friday 20 October 1874, at about four o'clock, Thomas Ramsay was taken from Crowle to be locked up at Epworth Police Station pending trial. About an hour after his arrival he ate a 'hearty' tea and appeared to be in good spirits. Mr. Snowden, Superintendent of Police, visited him between eleven and twelve o'clock that night and checked if Ramsay was warm and comfortable. He confirmed he was 'alright.'

At eight o'clock the next morning, the servant at the Police Station took Ramsay his breakfast – two rounds of bread and a pint of coffee. He too, reported finding Ramsay cheerful, although he only ate half a round of the bread. In the late morning the prisoner washed and walked about a bit and no one noticed anything unusual in his manner. At one o'clock, however, when Mr. Snowden took Ramsay his dinner, he found him suspended by the neck from the window bars of the cell by a silk handkerchief attached to his belt. He had wound the handkerchief twice around his neck. Mr. Snowden cut the body down immediately and carried it into the yard. Having laid it down, he examined the body and found it lifeless though still warm. Dr. Pullan came immediately but he, too, could offer no further assistance.

At the inquest, John Ramsay, the deceased's father, gave evidence of his son's state of mind. He reported that when he saw him at Crowle Police Station on the Thursday night he seemed in very low spirits and was wiping tears from his eyes. Despite the positive evidence given by all those who took charge of John, his father insisted that the signs of John's poor state of mind were evident for all to see. After carefully weighing up all the evidence the jury found the police had no case to answer and returned a verdict of 'suicide while in a state of temporary insanity.' Thomas' father argued vehemently over this assessment and pointed out that at the time of his arrest he wasn't a danger to anyone. He argued that had Thomas been allowed home on bail he would still be alive.

Suicides on the Isle continued on virtually an annual basis but from late 1900 to mid-1901 the rate increased dramatically when no fewer than five suicide attempts occurred in ten months. In October 1900 The Crowle Advertiser reported on a truly bizarre case of attempted suicide in Crowle. Alfred Mores from Manchester, lodging in a house in the town with two others, received a telegram from home at 11 p.m. After reading the telegram, he became very agitated, and for two hours paced the room, finally taking a knife from the mantlepiece and drawing it across his throat. His friends managed to wrestle the knife from him, but immediately he picked up another knife from the table and began stabbing at his body. Once again, his friends took hold of the knife, whereupon Mores grabbed the tongs from the fire grate and used them to strike himself over the head. When these too were prised from his grasp he made a lunge for the fire, attempting to thrust his head into the embers. All the time, Mores emitted strange guttural sounds and conversed in a 'rambling manner.' Dr. Alexander examined him after his arrest and believed him to be 'of unsound mind.' However, on the following morning when he examined Mores again, his opinion changed and he deemed him well enough to travel alone to Manchester. Mores showed genuine remorse for the damage he had done and swore it would not occur again. Alderman Blaydes of Epworth told the prisoner that if he was willing to pay for the damage caused he would dismiss the case. Mores agreed and left for Manchester with his brother. What the message in the telegram that sparked the incident said, remained secret.

The next suicide, in March 1901, involved Solomon Clark of Epworth who strangled himself in a closet at his lodgings. Two months later, thirty-eight-year-old Elisa Harrison, drowned herself in the house cistern. Elisa suffered from bouts of depression after losing a child to drowning in the same cistern a year earlier. The day before her fatal act she had stood in her garden and watched as a procession of school children passed the house. Her husband believed it was this that brought back memories of her accompanying the 'lost' child in the same procession the previous year. They were memories too painful to bear any longer. In July, when George Chant's attempt at suicide failed, magistrates dismissed the case against him when his son, also called George, promised to look after his father and ensure he did not repeat his 'crime.'

Finally, the most graphic account of a suicide in 1901 appeared in the October edition of the Sheffield Telegraph. Robert Cressey, a labourer from New Trent Cottages, Crowle, hung himself in a horse halter, suspended from a bacon hook in the kitchen ceiling. He and his wife Martha had gone up to bed at around 9 p.m., but the couple argued. Robert refused to get into bed with his wife and went off to get a rope, threatening to hang himself. Eventually, Martha talked him round and he got into bed beside her. He got up at 5 a.m. and she assumed he was going to work, but when a neighbour called round later, Martha spoke to him from an upstairs window. She told him she feared Robert had hung himself as she could see the shadow of his body reflected on the kitchen door. At first, she refused to come downstairs, but the neighbour persuaded her to open the door and let him in. Entering the kitchen, he came upon Robert's lifeless body swinging from a rope, the halter around his neck. He cut the body down and removed the halter before Martha could see the full extent of her husband's demise.

At the inquest, the jury heard how Cressey had been in Wadsley Asylum for a consierable time and had only been home for about seven weeks. During his time away, Martha had taken in a lodger and the family had 'increased by one.' Robert believed the lodger to be responsible for this and since then 'domestic life had been far from happy.' In a note left by the deceased, he wrote, 'Good morning to you and the children. It's all you Martha. God bless you all. Robert Cressey.' Although somewhat cryptic, the jury took the words to indicate those of a confused mind and, in this instance, as with all the other suicides that year, returned a verdict of 'suicide while temporarily insane.'

After a lull of six years, a spate of suicides again hit the headlines in the Isle. When Martha Ward of Belton set off to walk to Epworth, she little thought that on her return she would find her husband hanging in their kitchen. A year later, twenty-year-old Sydney Nutt left the Trent Wharf Hotel one evening saying he was going to commit suicide. No one believed him as he had threatened this on other occasions, but when he didn't appear next morning the police were informed and they began dragging the canal. They found his body under the bridge. Perhaps the saddest of all the suicides that occurred before the First World War, however, was that of seventy-year-old Bessie Pilsworth. In October 1913, she was elated to learn that, as from January the following year she would receive a pension. The extra money would help her and her husband face the future with optimism. So it proved until August when her husband received his pension and Bessie found hers reduced to 3 shillings. In her delicate condition, the bad news came as a 'hammer blow' and, unable to cope, she hung herself in the stable while her husband was at work. At the inquest, her husband told the jury that reducing her pension 'almost broke her heart.'

As if the horrors of the Great War were not hard enough to bear, suicides continued apace. In late January 1915, there came news of two unfortunate cases. The first one reported on the death of John Pettinger, a sixty-four-year-old bachelor of Sandhill Farm, Epworth. For some years his eccentric lifestyle and bouts of depression concerned several of his neighbours. Having seen some German prisoners in and around the town, John became convinced that a German invasion was underway. In the early months of the war, these prisoners were guarded but, when it became apparent they posed no danger to the local populace, some were allowed to live and work on farms with minimum supervision. They came and went at will; some becoming well-known faces around the town. John could not reconcile this, and on many occasions, he spoke of his fears, but it seemed no amount of reassurance could quell his anxieties. Late one night he left his cottage and walked along Scawcett Lane bound for the Folly Drain. Next day, on his way to work, Thomas Gravill found John's body face down in the water. When P.C. Sharman recovered the body he noted that John had on one unlaced boot, 'as though he had dressed hurriedly.' The other boot was missing and never found. Whether John slipped or pitched himself deliberately into the drain could not be determined as there were no marks along the drain bank to show if he had struggled to stop falling into the water or made a vain attempt to regain the bank. The Folly Drain was two miles from Sandhill Farm which for John would have constituted a considerable walk. There seemed no logical reason that he would be out and about so far from home and so late at night. Although he left no note, the inquest concluded that John had entered the water willingly and although this should have led to a verdict of 'suicide,' they spared the family any indignity by reaching a decision of 'found drowned.'

The second case involved Emma Robinson, a forty-two-year-old married woman from Crowle. Under arrest for drunkenness in

The River Torne, looking north from Scawcett Bridge.

Epworth, she was being taken to Hull gaol by P.C. Sharman and Mrs. Hill, the wife of Superintendent Hill of Epworth, to serve her sentence. The group left Epworth by train and arrived at Goole Station at 9.05 a.m. They were preparing to change trains when, without warning, and just as the Hull train approached, the prisoner jumped the three yards from the platform and lay with her neck on the rail. The episode happened so quickly no one had time to restrain her. Just before the engine and the first carriage went over her neck and decapitated her, Emma began laughing hysterically. Station staff placed Emma's body on a stretcher, covered it with sacks and organised its removal to the mortuary in Goole.

The jury learned that Emma had been in custody for several days and had been no trouble. In fact, she seemed resigned to her term in prison and had even been cheerful on the first leg of the journey, laughing and joking with her escorts. Emma, not handcuffed to either of her escorts was being conveyed in the accepted manner for female prisoners. Mr. Edward Shipman, stationmaster at Goole reported seeing the deceased jump deliberately in front of the Hull to Doncaster train and 'throw' herself down on the track. His evidence, and the reports of Emma's fiendish acceptance of her fate, saw the jury return a verdict of 'suicide whilst of unsound mind.'

The fear of being labelled 'a shirker' led to Charles Staniforth of Crowle feeling obliged to re-enlist in the army at the age of 37. Charles joined the East Yorkshire Regiment for twelve years in 1895 and fought in the Boer War. Invalided out of the army before the end of his service, he was not A1, but when Britain entered the Great War, he felt compelled to 'do his bit.' His decision went against the advice of his immediate family. The Army found him unfit for front-line duties, but such was the need for men, the authorities placed him in a labour battalion. On 1 December 1915, after spending several months in France he wrote home in a somewhat rambling tome:

Dear Father and all at Medge Hall just a few lines hoping they find you all in good health as they leave me middling only that I am stuffed up with cold and right hoarse. We have had a week of rather wintry weather snow and frost it is very cold here at nights we are on the top of a big hill ever so high but I like it better than where we were before we came here. I have not heard from Claude yet I wrote nearly a fortnight since but he has not written back he has never wrote to me yet and I don't think I shall write to him any more unless he writes and I have not heard from Tom since a long while before Claude came on leave but I hope they are both of them all right. I have just had a letter from Frank Burkinshaw I saw him just before we came here and he says I should see in the paper about (D) and Fred Chester being wounded but I have not received the paper with it in yet. Tell Ethel she is to send it every week and a letter too she has wrote to me more than any one yet though I had the Gazette week before last but no letter, so I think I have told you all with best love to you all I remain your son C. Staniforth.

p.s. we shall soon have Christmas now - I would like to have my dinner at home (there) but I begin to think I (shan't) but I hope to see you all soon.

Charles was to write another letter, thanking the ladies of Crowle for the parcel that contained the 'very things that are needed, especially the towel and socks, as we only have one towel and we have to do our own washing, and you cannot always get them dry as the weather out here is simply awful. We scarcely ever have a dry pair of socks on. I am in good health with the exception of a cold. I am in a labour battalion, as I am rather deaf.'

The Army discharged Charles in 1916, ostensibly for his defective hearing, though the family recognised he returned from France in a poor mental state. He went to live with his sister in Balby but seemed unable to shake off his dark moods. One day he walked out into the fields and didn't come back. His death at the age of 39, brought on by his depressed state, came as a great surprise to his friends in Crowle.

In the 1920s, Charles Birkinshaw, a quiet, unassuming, retired farmer of North Street, Crowle, was known and respected throughout the town. On Friday 15 July 1927, he walked with purpose some 150 yards into a cornfield owned by Frederick Smith, took out his pocket knife and cut his throat. It was an act that, to many, seemed entirely out of character and hard to explain. What few outside his close family realised was Charles had been deeply troubled for some time. Having lost his wife three years previously he had begun to suffer from bouts of depression and 'stomach trouble.' His brother, who lived at Hooton Pagnall, had stomach cancer at the time and this troubled Charles greatly. He saw his ailment as matching that of his brother and not wishing to endure a slow death, he resolved to commit suicide. He told his housekeeper that he thought he had 'something coming' and he didn't want to end up like his brother. He went on to say, 'he felt he should be obliged to make away with himself to get on top of his trouble.' The housekeeper thought little of it at the time and passed it off as idle chat. Next morning Charles rose at his normal time, ate a good breakfast and went for a walk at about 8.15 a.m. When he did not return for his lunch at 10.30 a.m. and missed his dinner two hours later, the housekeeper became anxious and reported his absence to Charles' youngest daughter. She and the rest of the family knew nothing of his whereabouts, so they organised a search. They found him in the cornfield lying on his right-hand side, with a ragged gash across his throat. The pocket knife was still in his hand. In his pocket, they found a note that read: 'What with trouble without and within, I can't live any longer. Forgive me. Oh! my poor head.'

There was some confusion over the site of the incident as he was found close to the border between Lincolnshire and Yorkshire. Eventually, the authorities decided his body lay just inside Yorkshire, so Sergeant Benson of Crowle called the police in Thorne to come and take charge of proceedings. At the inquest, the coroner confirmed the deceased had committed suicide, being troubled with his own stomach and the deteriorating condition of his brother. After expressing sympathy for the family, he delivered the now familiar verdict of 'suicide whilst insane.'

For one of the most difficult suicides to comprehend we have to return to 1901. Twenty-one-year-old Percy Hardy of Haxey, was young, fit and active, and had given no indication of his deteriorating mental health. Like many though, Percy chose the River Torne for his final act. When the police responded to the call, they found his body between Tunnel Pits and Scawcett. He had folded his clothes neatly on the bank, placing his pocket watch and penknife by the side, arranged as though for some form of ritual. In the pockets of his jacket, the police found eight notes, each one about the size of a modern-day credit card. The first was the customary, 'please try to forgive me' note addressed to his mother and father. Others seemed to be attempts to put his life in order. He wrote, 'the only thing that bothers me is to leave my dear sister

Agnes.' To her, he wrote: 'The cheque I gave you this afternoon is for you,' and to a Mr. Copeman: 'Please look after my sister's interests.' Another note said; 'I have paid Mr. Hill his rent to April. The crops are worth more than the rent.' Presumably addressed to his family, on a further piece of paper, was the instruction: 'Please take everything from the garden but the potatoes, they belong to Mr. Thomas Pearson of Belton.' Stranger yet was another note that said simply: 'Also owe for tillage.' A final one spoke of an unresolved debt: 'Mr. Parkin promised to give me five pounds but I never got it.' The circumstances seemed so strange that the coroner found no cause to issue the acknowledge conclusion of 'suicide while temporarily insane,' and instead resorted to the rather more pragmatic, 'asphyxia through immersion in water.'

In many of the above cases, the authorities did not attempt to understand the lives of these desperate people. Perversely, Victorian society aroused in many an excited curiosity when exposed to the details of well-publicised suicides. This prompted many to visit the sites where these deaths occurred and, once there, a type of sympathetic awareness led these voyeurs to try and tap into the impulses and imagery of the victim. In extreme cases, this 'visionary power' led to some trying to emulate the actions of an earlier victim. Such was the case in the Isle where years after the event many residents would relive each detail and even make special trips to visit and revisit the sites where some of the more prominent suicides took place.

CHAPTER ELEVEN

Fire and Flame

MISADVENTURE

Turbulent by nature and design, the men of Axholme did not take kindly to the strict discipline of their new rector, Samuel Wesley. They had fought against the Crown for over fifty years and resented the support this rash, hasty, and at times overdramatic rector gave to Royalist causes. Instead of gaining their respect he fostered their enmity and became the object of their ridicule. They determined to bring misery to his time in Epworth. Much of it was low-key disagreement but on occasions, their primitive passions spilt over into acts of violence. In 1702 evidence points to them setting fire to the parsonage and two years later, much of his crop of flax. Early in 1705, Samuel found his cows maimed and his dog left with an injured leg. His friends advised him to leave the town, but he refused saying, ' 'tis like a coward to desert my post because the enemy fire thick upon me. They have only wounded me yet, and, I believe, can't kill me.'

Later that year, on Wednesday 30 May 1705 a mob stood outside Epworth Rectory firing guns and banging drums. They arranged themselves beneath one of the windows intent on making a nuisance of themselves. Their actions came at a particularly bad time for the family as a few weeks earlier, Susannah had given birth, and Samuel had taken the baby to a neighbour to act as the nurse. Unfortunately, the nurse lay over the child in her sleep and suffocated the poor infant. When she woke to find the corpse beneath her, she ran with it to the Rectory and handed it to one of the servants, and from there it was thrown 'cold' into Susannah's arms 'before she was well awake.'

However, by far the worst 'trial' the family faced happened on a dark February night in 1709, when 'a fierce north-east wind went pricking o'er moor and fen.' It heralded one of the most 'celebrated' fires in the history of the world. In a small room beneath the straw roof, Mehetabel Wesley slept alone. Within an hour of midnight, she awoke to find embers from the burning roof falling on her bed. As the flames burnt her foot, she let out a cry of pain and ran to wake the rest of the family. At the head of the stairs on the second floor of the Rectory and deep asleep lay Wesley's maid and five of Samuel and Susannah's children. They woke to find the building alight. Samuel and Susanna searched the house and believing they and the nurse had collected all the children from the nursery, gathered the family outside. It was only when John cried for help from a first-floor window that they realised he was trapped inside. The story of John's rescue is well known and does not need repeating here but, with John safe, Samuel gathered his

The rescue of the young John Wesley from the burning parsonage at Epworth, Lincolnshire. Mezzotint by S.W. Reynolds after H.P. Parker.

family around him to thank God for saving all his eight children. 'Let the house go,' he declared, ' I am rich enough.'

What is less well known, however, is the story of the 1854 Rectory fire. On the morning of Sunday 12 February, a French nursemaid, partially suffocated by the smoke, woke to find the rooms on fire. She managed to remove the two young children who were in bed in the same room and took them to a safe place. She then woke the rector, Charles Dundas, and despite being unable to speak English, ran into the Market Place to raise the alarm and seek help. Those who responded joined with neighbours to form two lines across the road; one passing buckets of water from the wells at Rectory Cottage, the home of James Ross, the other passing back the empty ones. Their efforts brought the fire under control.

At the morning service in Church the next day, Reverend Dundas expressed his thanks to God and to all those who assisted and drew parallels with the Wesley fire - the month, the time of the discovery, the fact the maid raised the alarm, the help from locals and the safe delivery of all. On further exploration, he found the fire had started in an upper room where the joists underneath the fireplace ignited resulting in burning embers falling into the room below.

When, in 1732, another fire raged in Epworth and burnt down many buildings, stacks of corn and hay, several people wandered the neighbourhood begging under the pretence of their loss. It led to the authorities producing handbills and placing adverts in newspapers that everyone should ignore these 'imposters.' None of the sufferers had been allowed to 'go about and beg upon that account.' They had been told 'well disposed Christians would come to their aid when and where it may be thought proper.'

That fire was an ever-present danger in houses, chiefly constructed of flammable materials and illuminated by naked flames, was graphically illustrated in February 1744 in neighbouring Haxey. A fire that began close to the church spread so quickly that, in less than three hours, it consumed over sixty dwellings and a hundred and nineteen barns. Panic and pandemonium ensued, and such was the speed and intensity of the fire 'inhabitants were driven naked into the fields' to escape the inferno. Some folk ran into the open ground clutching whatever valuables they could muster. One widow arrived on Tower Hill with a chicken under each arm and refused to put them on the ground for fear they might run home and head back towards the fire. A disabled man arrived having been pushed to safety in a wheelbarrow! The more robust members of the community set up bucket brigades and although these had some effect on minor outbreaks, they had little impact on the overall magnitude. Investigators never established the cause of the fire but evidence pointed to it starting accidentally. Local authorities computed the cost of the damage at £10,000 (over three-quarters of a million pounds in today's money). The fire made headlines in national and provincial newspapers as far apart as Plymouth and Newcastle.

Depiction of the Haxey fire from the tapestry kneeler in St. Nicholas' Church, Haxey.

In Crowle too, on 10 September 1818, when a chimney caught fire, a high wind fanned the flames onto surrounding cottages. Had it not been for the exertions of neighbours and bystanders, the likelihood was that the fire could have spread on a similar scale to the one at Haxey. The three cottages destroyed belonged to poor people who were out at work when the alarm was raised. They returned to the charred remains destitute and reliant upon charity from the parish.

Even on the isolated farms of the Isle fire was a significant hazard, particularly at harvest time when the heat generated inside haystacks often caused them to ignite spontaneously. When winds blew across the Axholme plains and fanned the flames all the local fire brigades could do was try to stop the fire from spreading further. Many's the time the poor farmer had to stand and watch as his year's crop disintegrated in a matter of minutes.

The most significant problem in the Crowle area, however, was the danger posed by fire on the moors. These occurred at

Peat fires sweep across Crowle moors.

regular intervals in the early twentieth century with severe ones happening in 1909 (when some 500 acres ignited) and in 1911. In the latter instance, fanned by a strong wind, the fire spread rapidly across the moor engulfing the many stacks of dried turf. Men from Medge Hall joined the Crowle workforce in trying to bring the fire under control, but their efforts proved futile. They resorted to digging wide trenches to create firebreaks. Closer to the town and in line with the direction of the fire were some paraffin wells, and the fear was that if these caught fire little could be done to avert a major disaster. Thankfully, the fire burned itself out during the night and what could have been a devastating tragedy was averted.

In late 1890 a dreadful death from burning occurred at Owston Ferry. Seventy-five-year-old Tobias Broadbent went to bed with his invalid wife around seven o'clock on Christmas Eve. He got up about an hour later and in a confused state fell onto the fire which was about two feet from the bed. Two neighbours, James Mell and Jane Weatherhogg, were in the habit of checking on the couple and as they entered the house Weatherhogg turned to Mell and said, 'Dear me, what a smell of burning!' Entering the couple's bedroom, they saw Tobias lying on his left side across the hearth. His cotton nightshirt had been burnt off, and his flannel drawers were smouldering. Weatherhogg snatched a blanket from the bed and enveloping James in it managed to douse the flames. It seemed Tobias had struggled hard to save himself and his invalid wife must have managed to get out of bed to try and help him as the visitors found her laid holding Tobias' leg. She said she had tried to drag him from the flames but couldn't move him. Dr. Tickler came to dress Tobias' burns, but his attentions proved futile as Tobias died an hour later.

Two years later, the father of twenty-nine-year-old Elizabeth Temperton of Belton, heard his daughter screaming. Rushing into the kitchen, he found her sitting on the floor with her clothing alight.

Looking around he could not see how the accident happened, but as Elizabeth had been alone in the house, he guessed she must have reached across the fire to the mantlepiece and caught her dress in the flames. Using his bare hands and the kitchen rug, he managed to extinguish the flames, but the poor girl was so severely burnt she never regained consciousness and died the following day.

During World War One, John Dannatt of Sandbeds, Haxey, had just put some coal on his fire when the whole fireplace exploded in front of him. The blast was strong enough to blow John across the room causing severe burns to his face, throat, chest and hands. It wrenched two doors and a window out of their sockets and rendered serious damage to the ceilings of the house. Hearing the noise of the explosion, and seeing smoke billowing from the house, Mr. Kitchen, working on land nearby, rushed quickly to Dannatt's assistance. He managed to put out the clothing that was on fire and summoned medical aid. Some thought that Mr. Dannatt's poor eyesight had been a factor in him overlooking an unexploded cartridge that had found its way into the coal when delivered from the mine. Others, fearful of invading Germans, sought to blame 'Teutonic sabotage.' Dannatt made a painful and incomplete recovery but could remember nothing of the events that led to the explosion.

Around the same time, two men standing in the street in Garthorpe, noticed a strong smell of burning. Their search for the cause led them to the grocer's shop and post office belonging to Mr. G. W. Butterick. Finding the building well alight, they roused the family and got them to safety just as the flaming roof began to fall. Neighbours rushed to help, but a lack of water meant the best they could do was try to prevent further damage by dousing down the surrounding buildings. Butterick's stock of groceries and many of the fixtures and fittings, were reduced to a heap of smouldering rubbish. The Butterick's premises were only partially insured, and the family were left facing an expensive loss. There had been no fires or lights left on in the premises for almost a week, and the origin of the fire remained a mystery and a suspicious one at that!

In an appalling tragedy at Eastoft, eighty-nine-year-old Charlotte Holliday burned to death in her home. Her husband William, also eighty-nine, left the house at around 7 p.m. to visit a neighbour and when he returned half an hour later, he found the house full of smoke. Fearing his wife had possibly set something on fire in the bedroom, William stumbled along the passage to the bedroom, only to come across her body in flames on the floor. He raised the alarm and Mrs. Burkill, a neighbour, rushed to assist and did what she could, but the burns to Mrs. Holliday's body were so severe it proved impossible to save her. She had been partially paralysed for some years and had to be assisted into bed by her husband. On this occasion it seems she attempted to go to bed by herself and had fallen, dropping the lighted candle along the way. When the police moved her body, they found the candlestick beneath. At the inquest, conducted by Mr. P. A. Gamble, and upon the testimony of Dr. Alexander, the jury returned a verdict of, 'accidental death through shock caused by burns.'

There were many such household accidents in the early years of the nineteenth century, but none surpassed the one that befell the Vause family in Belton. Ephraim Vause and his thirty-year-old wife, Harriet, lived in a low thatched cottage on the west side of Westgate. Late one night, the pair realised their gilt pig was farrowing so they determined to sit up with it in case there were problems with the births. By early morning the pig had delivered a litter of seven pigs, four of which were born dead. The three survivors were quite frail and the morning being cold the Vauses decided to rotate bringing the piglets into the house to warm them. At intervals throughout the day, Ephraim, Harriet, their brother-in-law Thomas Leggott and his wife took it in turns to nurture the little pigs. At 1 a.m. the following morning it was Harriet's turn again; the Leggotts went home and Thomas took himself off to bed. Harriet placed the pig in a basket by the fire which she banked up before lying down on the sofa. The night was cold and unable to settle on the sofa, she got up, drew a chair in front of the fireplace and, placing the piglet in her lap, put her feet on the fender. Exhausted from the previous night's exertions, she was soon fast asleep.

About half-past four she awoke in pain to find her skirts scorched through and on fire. She ran to the door, but as she opened it, the inrush of wind fanned the flames causing them to rise and cover her body. Roused by her screams and not waiting to put on any clothes, Thomas dragged a blanket from the bed and rushed to her rescue. He succeeded in throwing the blanket over her, but as she threw up her arms to grasp him around the neck, the flames caught hold of the quilting, rising quickly to burn her shoulders and face. Thomas knocked her to the floor and rolled her in a carpet before tearing off all her clothes. The sight this revealed shocked him. So intense had been the heat that all across her body the burns were vivid red and her skin was blistering.

When Dr. Pullan arrived, Harriet's condition was deteriorating rapidly. He did what he could, applied salves to the burns and told Ephraim to keep her drinking water. He treated the wounds to Ephraim's hands and though he knew Harriet to be a strong woman he could offer nothing positive about her chances of survival. Harriet clung on to life for the next two days suffering untold agonies.

There is an Axholme saying that goes: 'Tis the thunder that frits, but t' lightning that strikes.' It was never more true than in July 1797, when during a severe storm, Mr. Oliver of Haxey and Mr. Huntington, an excise officer from Doncaster, took shelter under a tree in Haxey Garth. It would prove to be a disastrous decision. As the storm intensified, forked lightning lit the sky, and the earth seemed to shake from the deafening claps of thunder. Glad to have found a temporary shelter that would spare them from the intensity of the rain, the two men spoke in hushed tones and marvelled as the storm passed over them. Just as it seemed they had endured the worst, a bolt of lightning struck the tree. Mr. Oliver, leaning against the trunk of the tree had his coat sleeve and shirt torn from his arm, and the surge of electricity passing through his body demolished his shoes, melting the metal buckles. He died instantly. Hr Huntington fared better, receiving a shock which burnt his hand and side, fractured the glass of his pocket watch and left him stunned and unable to walk. It was quite some time before he managed to recover his senses and set off to find help. It was a salutary lesson of the dangers posed when sheltering beneath trees during a thunderstorm, but one that many neglected to heed.

In May 1865 another severe storm struck the Isle; lightning turned the sky a vivid purple, and there seemed no let up in the continuous roll of thunder. George Fawcett and Robert Coggan of Epworth, employed as piece workers gathering stones from the road near Vinegarth, were eager to get the job done, and both agreed to carry on through the storm. Suddenly, a particularly severe flash of lightning struck Fawcett to the ground where he lay stunned and immobile. He suffered a severe cut to the forehead, and scorching to the collar and front of his shirt appeared 'as though burnt in a fire.' The force of the strike even singed the hairs on his chest and forearms. Fawcett suffered, what the Stamford Mercury described as a 'multisystem dysfunction.' It led to a prolonged period of disability in which he suffered from fainting spells, erratic heartbeat, loss of muscle coordination and difficulties with speech. He vowed never again to work through a thunderstorm.

On the morning of 16 August 1875, William Taylor, owner of the mill on the hill approaching Westwoodside, could only stand by and watch as lightning struck the sails. One sail broke away from the main body of the windmill and another suffered damage in situ. Other buildings in the village suffered too. Edward Snowden saw several tiles on his roof destroyed as the lightning seared through the structure into the bedroom below. The bolt of electricity passed through the floor to the room below, destroyed a cupboard and set a pile of linen on fire. It then entered the wash-house, where Mrs. Snowden was busy with a washerwoman and demolished the water butt they were using to rinse the clothes. While neighbours helped put out the fires in the house, both women were treated for shock!

A year later another storm of similar severity broke over Epworth. The Epworth Bells reported that several homes in the town 'reverberated' under the force. The report stated that at the house of Mr. Newton in Chapel Street, 'the electric fluid seem[ed] to have entered the chimney above the roof, throwing down the chimney pot and stripping off a large number of tiles. It next passed into the attic, close to a bed where two of the youths of the family had slept the night before but were out when the storm came. Continuing its course, it passed down to the bedroom immediately below the attic, stripping wallpaper and plaster off the walls and ceiling in one corner, breaking glass in picture frames [and] scattering various articles about the room, which filled with smoke and the smell of sulphur.' The bolt of electricity left the room through a window, loosening the frame and breaking all eight panes. The Bells went on to report that: 'While all this was passing there was an invalid lady, a relative of the family, in the bed at the other end of the room. She was happily untouched, but was of course much alarmed by the shock!'

Perhaps the most extensive storm to hit the Isle occurred on 2 July 1893. Throughout the morning and early afternoon, dark clouds increased over the area and by quarter past five, at the height of the storm, vivid lightning and deafening thunder preceded severe rainfall that in minutes drew floods in the streets of most towns and villages. The lightning struck the home of John Coy of Epworth, splitting the beading around the fireplace in the bedroom, cracking the ceiling, tearing wallpaper from the walls and leaving a sulphurous smell. Downstairs the marble hearthstone split in two and soot covered the kitchen floor. The lightning splintered the wooden frame of a picture but left the glass undamaged.

At the conclusion of Epworth's Agricultural Show in 1873, the firework display, organised by Belle Vue Gardens of Hull, got out of hand. After two rockets lit up the sky and fuelled the expectations of a crowd in excess of 2,000, things started to go wrong. At first, several fireworks failed to ignite and then some went off out of sequence. This brought alarm to several bystanders and, even though they were in a roped off area ten yards away from the explosions, they began to move away to a 'more cautious distance.' The worst malfunction happened when one firework, described as a 'mortar,' slewed during ignition and discharged flames at head height. The force of the explosion hit 12-year-old Thomas Everatt full in the chest, blew off his left arm and caused severe burning to his head and neck. Although he received immediate aid, Thomas died fifteen minutes later, his last words being 'Oh dear!' To avoid a panic in the crowd, the organisers continued with the display – an act for which they received universal criticism. Thomas' funeral took place at the Baptist Church in Epworth a week later. At the inquest, the company denied all responsibility claiming the spectators were the prescribed distance away from the display and they could not entirely legislate for the 'capricious volatility of gunpowder.' The coroner criticised their decision to carry on with the display after Thomas' injury and death but did not hold the company to account over their safety procedures. He brought in a verdict of 'accidentally killed by a bursting mortar.'

CHAPTER TWELVE

Grave Mistakes and a Turbulent Priest

MISADVENTURE AND MAYHEM

When in 1874 Henry Keet requested a tombstone be placed on his daughter's grave in the churchyard at Owston Ferry, little did he realise he would set in motion a chain of events that would split the village, the nation and officers of the Anglican Church in England, and rumble on through the generations late into the twentieth century. Keet, described by his Methodist flock, as the Reverend Henry Keet, Wesleyan Minister, requested that these titles should be engraved into the stonework of the headstone along with the dedication to his daughter. It was a request, the vicar at St Martin's Church, Rev. George Edwin Smith, (with the support of churchwardens John Barnard and John Frewin and several parishioners) refused. Smith objected to Wesleyan preachers taking on the title of 'minister' and having the right to call themselves 'reverend.' In truth, he regarded the Wesley body as nothing better than schismatics, little more than a religious splinter group worthy of his contempt. As such he refused to deal with Keet directly and declared that all negotiations must be conducted through Mr. Barningham, the local stonemason.

When all attempts at compromise failed, Keet wrote to the Christopher Wordsworth, Bishop of Lincoln (the nephew of the poet William Wordsworth), to ascertain ecclesiastical law on the subject. The Bishop wrote back saying, 'it is the duty of the incumbent to examine epitaphs which it may be proposed to inscribe on tombstones in the churchyard of his parish; and that he is empowered by law to make objections to anything in them which in his judgment is liable to exception. What title should be given you by your co-religionists is not the point at issue, and I express no opinion on it. But the question is, whether the title reverend should be conceded to you on a tombstone by ministers of the Church of England, who are the responsible guardians of her churchyards. For such reasons as these I have abstained from giving the title of "reverend" to Wesleyan preachers, not (I need hardly say) from any feeling of disparagement towards them, but because I honour consistency and truth, and because I am sure they would despise me if I acted against my conscience, and were to practise that kind of liberality which courts popularity by giving away what does not belong to it.'

After reading the Bishop's carefully worded statement, Mr. Keet took the remedy open to anyone who wants to erect a memorial to the dead in church or churchyard, but who cannot get the incumbent's permission; he applied to the Consistory Court of the Diocese for a faculty. In this, he was assisted by the Wesleyan Conference, who appointed a committee to determine whether there was anything in the law that could compel the Vicar of Owston Ferry to admit the tombstone. If not, their remit was to 'take steps towards having the law altered.' Initially, they brought the case before Dr. Walter Phillimore, Chancellor of the Diocese of Lincoln. After some deliberation he backed the vicar's decision, alleging that to allow the inscription would be contrary to the laws of the Church of England. Phillimore cited the example of John Wesley himself who discouraged the terms 'revered' and 'minister.' If no less a worthy than Wesley treated these words with disdain, then the chancellor stated he could not recognise the right of Wesleyan preachers to claim them. It was, he said, against the spirit of the law, the Canons and the Book of Common Prayer.

No sooner had the decision been conveyed than it was taken up by Mr. Brooks, counsel for Mr. Keet. It was he who gave notice that the case would be put before the Court of Arches, an appeal court of the Archbishop of Canterbury, dating back to the thirteenth century. This action would be expensive, but Brooks acted in the knowledge that several wealthy Wesleyans were prepared to cover any expenses incurred.

The Epworth Bells reported the story in a somewhat disdainful manner, believing it to be 'the first time in England wherein a tombstone has been kept out of a churchyard on the grounds referred to.' The report went on: 'It may throw some light on the matter to mention that in the churchyard of Epworth no such question is raised, and any visitor to Epworth churchyard will find more than one tombstone whereon "Reverend" and "Minister" are inscribed as the designation of Wesleyan preachers. But at Epworth, the law of courtesy decides the question.' It is possible the reporter was referring to the tombstone of Richard Smailes, a Wesleyan minister who died in 1865 and whose epitaph included both the contentious titles.

The Cornish Telegraph went further saying, 'shall Nonconformists be regarded as fellow Christians, and their clergy as fellow labourers: or shall the cry of schism still be continued. If the latter, who are the schismatics? Certainly not the Wesleyans, if the scriptures are to be accepted before Lincoln orthodoxy and Mr. Phillimore's opinion. Schism is breaking away from the "unity of the spirit" – refusal to accord that fellowship and charity which common sense at last must admit are the bonds of true brotherhood. The schismatics, then, are the Bishop of Lincoln and his co-religionists.' The Times said that the decision was 'in the highest degree insulting to a religious body which has earned for itself a high place among the denominations of the country.'

To the surprise of many, the Archbishop of Canterbury pronounced strongly in favour of allowing the erection of the tombstone. Even so, the Bishop and the rector persisted in their desire to ban Keet's gravestone from the churchyard. It was only when the Wesleyan Committee of Privilege communicated their intention to place the matter before Parliament, that the bishop, finding himself in an untenable position wrote to the rector of Owston Ferry advising 'retreat' over the matter. Yet again, the rector refused to yield, stating his determination to 'drive away all heresy from his parish!'

The sorry saga ended when the contentious words 'reverend' and 'minister' were placed before the Privy Council. The council overturned all previous decisions and ruled that the Established Church had to concede in law they did not have exclusivity over these terms. They went further, stating there was 'ample authority for applying the word "minister" to teachers and preachers outside the pale of the Establishment.' Regarding the term 'reverend,' the argument centred on the known fact that, until recent times parochial clergy had been addressed by the honorific title 'Sir' even though they had not received a knighthood. Equally, laymen, women and judges had been known to take on the titles of 'reverend,' 'right reverend,' and 'worshipful' - again, there was no exclusivity over these salutations.

In March 1876, with the issuing of a faculty for the erection of the tombstone, Mr. Keet finally saw the matter of his daughter's gravestone resolved. The vicar of Owston Ferry did not appear to defend his conduct when legal expenses were set at £1,600 (some of the more ill-informed newspapers such as 'The Scotsman' reported the figure to be £16,000). In a letter to Mr. Barningham, Keet explained his 'wish for it to be done in a quiet manner,' so his sympathisers would not turn the event into a further demonstration. So it was that soon after nine o'clock, on a bright April morning, Mr. Barningham began transporting the headstone up the street toward the churchyard. Immediately this attracted a crowd, and there were some unpleasant scenes before it arrived there. Mr. Keet did not attend the installation and unsurprisingly, neither did Rev. Smith! Rev. J. Charlesworth, the new Wesleyan Minister and one or two members of the Wesleyan Society at Ferry supervised its erection

The fallout from this sorry episode had far-reaching consequences. The Rev. G. W. Manning rector of St. Petrock Minor near Padstow, known for his eccentricities, announced he would no longer open letters addressed to him in the 'now desecrated title of reverend!' One of Manning's eccentric acts was to sleep in a coffin he had made for him to prepare himself for his final rest. He stored the coffin beneath his bed!

Some months later, when another interment took place close to the 1828 Wesleyan headstone of William Howkins, and in what was a flagrant act of revenge, the vicar had it placed so it obscured the Methodist wording. Traditionally, when stones were set close together, one would be reversed to ensure both inscriptions were visible. One positive to come out of what became known as 'The Scandal of Owston Ferry's Tombstone' was a relaxation in the 'rules' concerning Church of England graveyards. Four years later, when a Roman Catholic man died in Epworth, the family opted for Rev. Canon Gordon the Catholic priest of Crowle, to conduct the service. Although they had not applied through the channels of the 1857 Burials Act, Rev. Dundas of Epworth consented. His decision saw a Roman Catholic priest officiate at the church in Epworth for the first time since the Reformation.

The Bishop of Lincoln went on to invite the Wesleyans over the Owston Ferry incident to a 'friendly conference' attended by three chaplains and a lay friend. He met a former President of the Wesleyan Conference, some ministers and other members of the connection and explained to them his views on the relationship of 'Wesleyanism' to the Church. He referred to what John and Charles Wesley had said and written on the subject and proposed terms for a closer union. He requested that his paper might be communicated 'with his respectful compliments' to the President of the Wesleyan Conference based on what he believed to be fundamental principles of the Church of England. He spoke of his admiration for Wesleyan Methodists, of their zeal and energy and his feelings of Christian charity towards them. Neither party accepted his paper; it would take decades of ecumenical dialogue before leaders of the Anglican and United Methodist Churches began to work towards full communion between the two churches.

The 'final' resting place for Annie Keet's headstone in the churchyard at Owston Ferry.

When the local authority closed the old part of the graveyard, allowing it to become 'God's Acre,' they moved the tombstone outside the confines of the graveyard and placed it close to the lychgate. Here, it suffered considerable damage so in 1988 the Owston Ferry Historical Society paid for it to return to the churchyard. On 31 January, the vicar of Owston Ferry and the Wesleyan Minister came together to bless the stone in its new position. It marked the end of the sorry saga and pointed the way to far happier relations between the two denominations. Today, although the stone shows signs of age and damage, the inscription can still be read; it says:

In Sacred Memory of Annie Augusta Keet
Younger daughter of The Rev'd H. Keet
Wesleyan Minister
Died May 11th 1874
Aged 7 years and 9 months
'Safe shelter from the storms of life.'

In 1900, Belton Parish Council appointed a committee to look into allegations of irregularities over burials taking place in the churchyard. The sexton admitted that he had disinterred remains while preparing graves in the old church ground for future interments. He declared it impossible to dig a grave there without disturbing coffins and remains. He admitted that two people buried recently were left in ground only two feet deep as he had encountered other coffins at that depth. Pressed to explain further he spoke of one occasion when he had chopped off the side of a closed coffin and had laid this to one side. After the funeral he confessed to replacing it surreptitiously. In another more shocking revelation he recounted the time when digging a grave he unearthed a significant jumble of human remains. Placing these against the church wall, he covered them with earth to hide them from those attending the funeral. Unfortunately, on the day of the funeral, much of the earth had 'slipped,' and a gruesome sight awaited the mourners. After the interment, the sexton threw these remains unceremoniously back into the grave. It appears he did not complete the job successfully as some remained among the earth to be carted away and mixed with gravel to effect repairs in a farmer's yard! Despite cautioning the sexton for his 'misdemeanours,' the council recognised the shortcomings of the current churchyard and agreed unanimously to apply to the Secretary of State for an order to close the area.

At the outbreak of the English Reformation, England had ten hermitage-monasteries. Commonly called 'Charterhouses,' a corruption of the French name 'Chartreuse,' these institutions were held in the highest esteem. As a result, King Henry VIII set out to win them over in his bid to legitimise his marriage to Anne Boleyn. In mid-April 1533 he ordered Augustine Webster, the prior of Melwood, to swear to the Oath of Supremacy. On four occasions Webster refused to accept the King, his sovereign lord, as the supreme head of the Church. Unable to compromise his calling, Webster determined, along with John Houghton, prior of London's Charterhouse, to petition Cromwell for an exemption from this royal decree. Cromwell refused to listen, in fact, he had them arrested and placed in the Tower of London. On 20 April he questioned Prior Webster, who once again, declared that he could not compromise his faith and take the oath. Along with Prior Houghton and Dr. Reynolds, a Brigittine monk of Sion, Webster was charged with treason eight days later. All pleaded 'not guilty' and were led back to prison to await the decision of the jury.

As the jury's deliberations dragged on, Cromwell fearing they might find the men innocent, 'urged' the jury to bring in a verdict of guilty. On 4 May 1535, despite Archbishop Cranmer intervening

On 4 May the Church of Holy Souls in Scunthorpe organises an annual pilgrimage to Melwood Farm, Owston Ferry, in honour of St. Augustine Webster.

on their behalf, the Carthusian priors and Dr. Reynolds were drawn through the streets of London on hurdles to face public execution at Tyburn. Here, 'without respect for their Order' archives in the Vatican tell of the men being 'hanged with great ropes. While they were still alive, the executioner cut out their hearts and bowels and burned them. Then they were beheaded and quartered, and the parts placed in public places on long spears. [It] is believed that each one saw the other's execution fully carried out before he died – a pitiful and strange spectacle, for it is long since persons have been known to die with greater constancy. No change was noticed in their colour or tone of speech, and while the execution was going on they preached and exhorted the bystanders with the greatest boldness to do well and obey the King in everything that was not against the honor of God and the Church.'

CHAPTER THIRTEEN

In Cold Blood

MURDER

Early on the morning of 21 October 1869, William Daniel Webb a forty-three-year-old lodging-house keeper from Epworth, was in bed with his wife when she told him she was pregnant. Refusing to believe the child was his, Webb got up and went into an adjoining room where he picked up a hammer. He returned to his wife and seeing her trying to get up, he pushed her down onto the bed and struck her several blows on the head that rendered her unconscious. A newspaper report stated her head was 'fearfully lacerated and the bedclothes saturated with blood.' Believing his wife to be dead, Webb left the house. He was not seen again until he arrived at the police station with his throat cut. He told the officer in charge to arrest him as he had killed his wife for being unfaithful. Unknown to him, in the time between his attack and his arrival at the police station, his son had called the doctor and the police. They found the unfortunate lady in a bad state but alive. When the officer told Webb his wife was not dead, Webb replied, 'Oh but she will die, it is impossible for her to live! I must be locked up.' He stated further that he had 'cut his throat in a nice quiet spot away from Epworth' so that he might bleed to death. When this did not happen, he decided to surrender to the police.

The magistrate placed him on remand to await trial in Epworth gaol. One cold night he asked the police constable on duty if he could warm himself by the fire. The constable agreed and the two spent some time chatting in front of the fire. When the time came for Webb to return, he entered the cell then feigned a collapse. As the constable entered the cell to check on him, Webb jumped up and closing the door behind him, made his escape by locking the confused constable inside. The policeman remained locked in the cell until his relief arrived three hours later. In circulating Webb's description, the police made much of the substantial amount of sticking plaster covering the cut across his throat.

Webb was 'on the run' for several weeks when in bizarre circumstances the officer who had been imprisoned by Webb was fetching water from his yard when he saw him pass the house. He followed him for some time and when confronted, Webb told him he was in Epworth to give himself up! When the case came to trial, the judge sentenced Webb to fifteen years penal servitude, commenting on his 'precarious state' and remarking that it was providence that had saved his wife's life. Morally, the judge concluded, Webb was guilty of murder and such a sentence was completely justified. It turned out that Webb's suspicions about his wife's infidelity were groundless!

In a similar incident some years later, fifty-four-year-old James Anderson, one-time landlord at a public house in Owston Ferry, murdered his wife, Mary, by stabbing her in the neck with a pen knife and then used it to cut his own throat. The Anderson family lived at East Ferry in a 'clean little cottage.' It was not a happy or harmonious household. James had been a drunkard for some years and, after a series of disagreements, had already taken his son to court in Gainsborough on a charge of assault. Following this, Mary Anderson left the family home to live with her sister across the river in Owston Ferry. Mary's nephew, John Wood, lived with family in East Ferry and it was he who Anderson sent across the river to tell Mary he wished to speak to her on business. Mary saw this as an opportunity to bring some of her clothes back to Owston Ferry. Soon after she arrived, the couple quarrelled loudly. The noise alerted and Wood, who rushed into the room just in time to see Anderson draw a knife from his pocket. As man and wife struggled on the kitchen floor, Wood ran to get help. Having done so he made his way back to the house where he met his aunt staggering down the street with a huge gash in her neck from which blood 'flowed copiously.' He saw her rest briefly against a gate before two men assisted her towards the village inn. As they reached the entrance, Mary fell down and although the men tried to raise her to her feet she remained on the floor. Rushing back to the house, Wood found Anderson hacking at his throat with the same knife he had used on his wife. As the youngster looked on in horror, Police Constable Jackson, entered the house and both watched as Anderson collapsed face down to the kitchen floor. When Dr. Pope and Dr. Tickler arrived they found Anderson unconsciousness. They took this opportunity to stitch up the wound. P.C. Jackson found a loaded revolver on the mantlepiece and when he asked Wood if he knew anything about it the boy confirmed that the gun had been in the house for some time. He remembered Anderson loading it the previous night as he feared someone was outside. P.C. Jackson concluded that this was a ruse and he had loaded the gun in preparation for the arrival of his wife. For some reason he had opted to use his penknife instead.

Anderson made a slow recovery from his wound and was able to stand trial. The jury took little time in finding him guilty. Sent to gaol in Lincoln, Anderson chose execution over transportation. On the morning of 19 February 1883, after waking early on the day of his execution, Anderson received a visit from a Wesleyan minister. Following a 'hearty' breakfast he received the sacrament and 'cheerily' underwent the pinioning of his arms. At 9 o'clock, he walked firmly to the scaffold erected close to his cell. The government executioner, William Marwood, adjusted the cap and rope then pulled the lever. Marwood had calculated for an eight-foot drop which proved sufficient to cause an instantaneous death.

It would be one of the last executions for the man who, in a nine-year career hanged 176 people. Marwood invented the technique known as the 'long drop,' which ensured a prisoner's neck would break as the rope reached its limit - a more humane method than strangulation. Immediately after the execution, the authorities hoisted a black flag from the clock tower of the prison.

When John Dean, Charles Brown, Charles Robinson and John Sharp went into the River Don Inn in Eastoft for their usual quart of beer they were expecting a quiet drink. There were several Irishmen in the pub, many in a noxious state of inebriation. Often called 'scratters,' these Irishmen turned up in the north of the Isle to work on the farms. Some would drink so heavily that they had spent almost all their week's earnings by Sunday night. On this night, Patrick (Paddy) Welch, was sat by the fireside in an armchair as if asleep. John Connelly, a friend of Welch, told Brown to wake him so he could buy him a pint. Brown went up to the sleeping man and stroked the side of his face. When Welch did not respond Brown pulled his nose telling him to 'wake up and have a sup of beer.' Waking in an angry mood, Welch said, 'thou'd better give over or I'll into thee,' to which Brown retorted, 'I think thou will't not Pat.' This spat soon developed into a row between the Irish and the British and when things looked like getting out of hand the landlord asked Brown and his friends to leave the pub. As, they did so an Irishman called Kelly began to goad Welch into action. He did not take much persuading and left the pub to confront Brown. When Brown saw him approaching, he said, 'Will ta into me now?' Welch answered, 'I will if you don't keep off.' The two men scuffled for several seconds before Brown staggered off and fell against the wall of a house. As the Irishmen left the scene, hurling stones as they went, Brown told his father he thought he was going to die and wanted to be taken home. His friends went to lift him, only to find he had received three stab wounds, two to the abdomen and one towards the groin. One of the wounds was so extensive his bowels protruded through his flesh. As he lay dying the police went in search of Welch. They found him leaning against a gate with blood on his hands and coat and two knives in his pockets. Somewhat surprisingly they took him to confront the dying man. When he saw the dying Brown, Welch burst out laughing.

At his trial in Lincoln for the wilful murder of Charles Brown, Welch pleaded 'not guilty.' After hearing from several witnesses, the judge directed the jury to discount murder as there was insufficient evidence as to who struck the first blow. He directed the jury to consider a reduced charge of manslaughter. The jury returned their verdict of guilty to the charge of manslaughter within a few minutes of retiring. Thanking the jury for their prompt but considered response, the judge sentenced Welch to seven years penal servitude.

The behaviour of Irish workers would cause problems for the Isle constabulary for many years. When several 'rough Irish gentlemen' entered the Mariners' Arms in Keadby and threatened the landlord and landlady with violence, the pair left the bar and summoned the constable. Meanwhile, the gang found their way into the cellar and began drinking freely. By the time the constable arrived, they had started fighting amongst themselves. Taking hold of each one individually the constable dragged them out of the pub and threw them over a fence. When one removed his belt and attempted to strike the constable across the face with the buckle, he stepped aside and with one blow knocked the Irishman out. It was just one of many occasions when the redoubtable local bobbies had to confront the drunken behaviour and foul language of these hard-living citizens from the Emerald Isles.

Samuel and Frances Barrowcliffe of Westwoodside had been married fourteen years and had four children. In the last few weeks of their marriage, they had not been living in harmony. On 9 July 1894, they were at Westwoodside Feast together and when Frances grew tired and asked Samuel to take her home. He refused and left on his own. Frances arrived some time later, having been escorted home by 'someone else.' A week later, when Samuel came back from work about 6.30 p.m., he began swearing at his wife, asking if she had had any of her fancy men there that day. Having eaten his tea, Samuel jumped up from the table and with a knife in his hand advanced toward his wife in a threatening manner. Frances clutched their baby in her arms and ran into the coal house and locked the door. Samuel followed her, and when he found the door barred, he ran back to the house and picked up his loaded gun. Frances took the opportunity to make good her escape. Seeing her getting away, Samuel raised the gun to his shoulder and fired, shouting, 'I will stop you this time.' Some of the shotgun pellets struck Frances on the back and down the right side of her head. Fortunately, she was some forty yards away from the house and was not seriously injured.

She managed to get into the house of Annie Bellamy and told her of the shooting. Annie went outside and found Samuel standing with his gun. 'You ought to be ashamed of yourself,' she told him,' I thought you would never shoot a woman.' 'I have been out shooting vermin,' replied Samuel, as he began loading his gun; 'I'll shoot you if you come into the street.' He went on to threaten anyone who came out of doors and said that if he saw his wife, he would 'blow her brains out.' Later, he claimed that, had his wife not had the baby in her arms, he would have 'sent her head to one side of the street and her body to the other.'

When P.C. Good arrived on the scene, he went to the Barrowcliffe's house and took possession of the gun which he found loaded and capped. He took the cap off and put the gun outside. He heard Samuel call out from upstairs 'Who's that?' P.C.

Good identified himself, whereupon Samuel came downstairs saying, 'I expect you've come for me?' Arresting Barrowcliffe, Good charged him with intent to murder and common assault. 'I am innocent of that charge,' countered Barrowcliffe.

At his trial at Lincoln Assizes, Samuel pleaded not guilty. The judge asked the prosecutor, Mr. Cracroft, if he intended to continue with the count of attempted murder to which Cracroft replied that all he wanted was justice and 'if your Lordship thinks there is no evidence to go before the jury on the charge of felony then I will proceed with the charge of common assault.' After consulting with his counsel, Samuel pleaded guilty to assaulting his wife and asked for mitigation towards his sentence. He had already been in gaol for five months awaiting trial, and during this time Frances had found it a struggle to maintain her children. Throughout the proceedings, she claimed to have never been afraid of the prisoner and was willing to live with him again. The judge called Frances to the bar, and in a tearful state, she said she would very much like to live with her husband as she had no other means of supporting the children. It seemed that both husband and wife were happy to let bygones be bygones. The judge informed Samuel that because of his 'hasty temperament' keeping a shotgun was a bad idea and, if released, he would expect Samuel to dispose of it. Samuel's name does not appear in the press again, so presumably, he took the advice of the judge.

CHAPTER FOURTEEN

Found Drowned

MISADVENTURE

Drowning is the third leading cause of unintentional injury, accounting for 7% of all deaths worldwide. In a watery area such as the Isle this percentage rises by several points. On 18 August 1791, the body of a man snagged on some branches along the banks of the River Trent close to Gunthorpe. It was in such a putrid state, having been in the water 'quite some time,' that identification seemed impossible and so it proved. The only clue to the man's profession was a two-foot rule found in his pocket. This object led the coroner to conclude that he may have been a mechanic on one of the river craft. In a bizarre verdict, the jury concluded that the man entered the water willingly and inexplicably opted for the cause of death being due to lunacy! It was not the first drowning in this most baleful of rivers, but it was one of the first recorded in a newspaper report.

Early on a Thursday morning in March 1892, young Freeman Smith, a farm boy at Tunnel Pit Farm, was on his way to work. As he approached the bridge between Poles Bank and Tunnel Pits he saw some clothing in the drain. Not sure what to make of this, Freeman ran to the farm and told Mr. Hill, the owner. Hill told him to take a rake from the yard and go and fish the clothes out of the water. On his first try, Freeman connected with the clothes but was unable to pull them to the side. He called the help of a man passing by and together they hauled the clothes in to the bank, only to find they covered the body of a woman. Running back to the farm in 'somewhat of a state,' Freeman spluttered out the discovery

The drain along Poles Bank Road.

to his master. He had hardly managed to get his breath back before Hill sent him to Epworth to inform the police.

It was P.C. Tomblin who heard the boy's story and straight away dashed to the scene on his bicycle. When he got to Poles Bank, he found the body had been removed to Wroot by the parish constable (the event had occurred just inside Wroot Parish). Back on the bicycle, Tomblin peddled furiously down the road to Wroot. He caught up with the constable just as he was about to examine the body. Together they searched for incriminating evidence but found none - there were no marks of violence. In the pockets of the clothing, they found 1s 7d and a pedlar's certificate belonging to fifty-one-year-old Sarah Brady. The document, dated 22 July 1891, showed its place of issue as Stanhope, County Durham.

Tomblin set about widening his search for evidence. Close to the site of the tragedy he came across a hawker's basket in which was food and a few personal items. He also discovered that a woman answering Sarah's description had been seen seeking lodgings at

Epworth the previous evening, but because of her presenting 'under the influence', she was repeatedly refused. He ascertained, further, that she had been seen late on the road from Epworth Turbary to Tunnel Pits in an advanced state of intoxication. All the evidence pointed to Sarah missing her footing as she crossed Poles Bank Bridge and the coroner agreed when issuing his verdict of 'found drowned.' Epworth police carried out extensive enquiries at Stanhope and throughout Durham County in the hope of discovering some of her relatives but learned nothing more. It was as though Sarah Brady had never existed!

When forty-five-year-old William Graham left the Bridge Inn at Belton late one night without ordering a drink, he seemed 'lost within himself.' He set off down Westgate towards the Sir Solomon Inn where he had been staying. William was a travelling musician and had spent much of the day in Crowle where he had entertained the residents on his banjo. Those in the town who heard him play spoke of the 'merry manner' in which he played, bringing joy to all who stopped to listen. The next morning James Arrand, crossing a field close to the River Torne, saw a body floating in the water in a 'mushroom position with the legs and head in the water and part of the back out.' James called for help and when another man arrived the two pulled the body out. James described it as 'cold and almost stiff.' It was the body of William Graham. P.C.Smith, who appeared shortly after thought the body had been in the water for about four to five hours. He found no marks on the banks to suggest the deceased had struggled on entry or attempted to exit the water. In William's pockets were a pipe, a spoon, a collecting bag and a pocketbook. P.C. Smith's immediate thought was that Graham had been sitting on the bridge and then fallen in the river.

At the inquest, the jury heard evidence that Graham appeared to be a man of 'high culture' and a 'most agreeable person.' He had left his banjo in the stables at the Sir Solomon where he had slept for the past fortnight. What could not be explained was why James Arrand found the Graham's body in the opposite direction to which he had left the Bridge Inn. The jury returned a verdict of 'Found Drowned' as there was insufficient evidence to determine whether the death was accidental or suicide.

Alfred Fearnley an itinerant, casual labourer of Ackworth but formerly of Crowle, arrived in Keadby about one o'clock. Fifty-years-old and unmarried, he was out of work and homeless. After spending time with family relations and friends, he ended up 'touring' the local hostelries. He had a bottle of stout at one club and a pint of beer at another. At 6 p.m. he went to the Mariner's Arms before heading for the Friendship Hotel. Here, he drank two pints of beer and then asked the landlord if he would take care of his watch and chain until he came back. It was a strange request, but the landlord agreed. Fearnley then had another bottle of stout and a glass of beer, before leaving the hotel at about 9.30 p.m. Half an hour later, George Elcock, an engine driver at Keadby, signed on for work at the engine sheds. Walking up the line to his engine, George heard someone shout, 'Where am I?' Looking up he saw a man on the left side of the bridge. The man said he wanted to be at Crowle, so George took him to the wicket gate leading to the towpath alongside the canal. Later George saw the man going in the wrong direction and fearing he might fall in the canal he set him on the right path again. The man did not engage in conversation, just walked away leisurely. George noted that the man did not appear drunk but he found the encounter 'disturbing.'

As P.C. Cowling reached the canal on his late night beat he noticed a body lying at the side of a pond. Nearby was his neatly folded jacket, with his hat placed on top. Upon searching the body, Cowling found 8d in coppers, a knife, a pipe and an insurance card. The card identified the body as Alfred Fearnley. Called to examine the body, Dr. Crowden of Keadby found a slight bruise on the bridge of the nose, but it was not consistent with a blow to the head. There were no signs of violence on the body or at the scene. The cause of death he gave as 'asphyxia through emersion in water,' and all indications led to what he described as a 'tranquil' death. Alfred's body was removed to Crowle and interred in the cemetery.

A year later, the body of Frederick Major Dobson was seen floating in the River Trent. Only a young man, Frederick had been missing from home for a day. The gruesome task of recovering the body fell to the ferryman. At the coroner's inquest, those called to give evidence spoke of the deceased's habit of going to the river bank to draw water for drinking in a pint mug. This revelation surprised the coroner who went on to state that Owston Ferry would never get a proper supply of drinking water if residents persisted in taking water from the river. The jury brought in an open verdict as there was no evidence to show how the deceased had entered the river. One juror, however, suggested that if the practice of taking water from the river persisted then perhaps the authorities should consider providing steps!

Whether or not there were steps in place by 1914, they would have had little bearing on the death of four-year-old Rupert Fletcher, son of George Fletcher, a village cab proprietor. Rupert was last seen at 4 p.m. on Monday 27 April, throwing sticks into the water from the jetty at Leggott's wharf. Although dragging operations continued until midnight the tide was strong, and those involved believed it would carry the body a great distance. The only explanation for his disappearance was that Rupert must have fallen in when playing on the wharf. Although his family and friends carried out an extensive search, they never found Rupert's body.

Even during the sad times of the First World War, the river kept up its rapacious quest for victims. In 1916 the coroner delivered verdicts on two young boys, both victims of drowning in the river. In the first tragedy, the five-year-old son of Fred Brown, a wagoner from East Butterwick, had gone off to play with his sister. When she returned without him, her explanations about what had happened were confusing. She said she had not seen her brother fall in the river but did not worry when she could not see him as she assumed he had set off for home without telling her. Next morning, after many hours searching, it was his father who found the young boy's body at a drain head. The poor boy's hands and much of his face had been eaten away by rats.

Within a day of this gruesome discovery, Mr. Thursby, a Stockwith boatman, recovered the body of four-year-old William Seth Garratt who had fallen into the Trent some months previously. He, too, had been playing with his sister. She reported seeing her brother placing his foot in the water and saying, 'I wish a big fish would come and bite my toe off.' As he stretched his leg further toward the water, little William slipped and fell into the river.

The tragedy did not satisfy the Trent's greed for willing victims, however, and throughout the rest of the twentieth century, it continued to demand (and receive) its share. In 1926 George, the nine-year-old son of Police Constable Cook of Owston Ferry, drowned in the river while fishing with a companion. It was a time when the river held significant stocks of fish and boys fishing along the banks were a familiar sight. George's hook caught on some stones, and as he leant over to free it, he overbalanced and fell into the river. He was swept away before his companion could raise help.

Three years later the body of an unknown male baby washed up on the bank close to the Crooked Billet. Dr. Erdheim attended the scene and deduced that death had taken place some twenty hours after birth and believed the body could have been in the water for up to two months. When pressed, he felt he could not say whether the child was dead or alive at the time of its immersion. As will be revealed in a later chapter, over the years the Trent offered itself as a useful receptor when girls and young women sought the disposal of unwanted infants!

At an inquest in 1939 into the drowning of Raymond Spencer, a sixty-year-old bachelor from the village, the coroner returned a verdict of 'Death by Misadventure.' The chief witness to the tragedy, Robert Tye of Cleethorpes recalled sailing his yacht along the river and seeing what looked like a man asleep on the river bank in a 'treacherous spot.' Having passed by, he heard a splash followed by shouts and saw Raymond thrashing in the water. Tye and a companion jumped into the yacht's rowing boat and headed in Raymond's direction, but could not reach him before he disappeared beneath the water. The men circled the spot for several minutes but saw no further sign of the body. Raymond's brother, George, testifying at the inquest, said he could think of no reason why Raymond would take his own life as he was 'as happy as a king.' Before closing the inquest, the coroner thanked Tye for his efforts in trying to effect a rescue.

CHAPTER FIFTEEN

They are in Heaven

MURDER

In 1834 the British Parliament reformed the Poor Law because of concerns over its rising cost. Part of this revision centred on laws relating to unmarried mothers and their illegitimate children. Previously, they had been legally entitled to receive support from the fathers of their children, but many reasoned that women would be less likely to engage in premarital sexual relationships if the outcome left them solely responsible for the support of the resultant child. Now it became the decision of a court, and not all cases went in favour of the woman. The magistrate's court in Epworth heard bastardy cases at 10.30 a.m. every other Thursday. Here, a member of the Board of Guardians could initiate a bastardy hearing to determine the rightful father and subsequently impose a weekly charge on him for the infant's support until the child was employable. Reported in the Epworth Bells, these cases were often brief with a simple statement to the effect that 'three bastardy cases were heard' being not uncommon. Any lack of success left many young women with only one avenue available – the workhouse.

No longer a matter dealt with by the Church, when the system failed and often to avoid 'double shame,' women delivered of illegitimate children resorted to the extreme measure of infanticide. They gambled on the sympathy of the court on what, throughout the rest of the century, became a politically delicate question. When the time came to deliver a verdict, the jury often swayed towards leniency especially if the evidence helped them declare the perpetrator 'temporarily insane.'

The earliest reference in the press of child murder in Axholme came in the July 1793 edition of The Stamford Mercury. The murder was not part of some collective grievance, but the cold-blooded murder of a female child by Elizabeth Richardson of Belton. Elizabeth was a twenty-one-year-old, unmarried mother reviled and scorned by many in the village. She elicited little sympathy for her situation having attempted to conceal her shame. There were some who thought that during her confinement she was already contemplating ridding herself of the child, whether by strangulation and casting the body on the nearest dunghill or tossing it into the river. The jury saw her actions as a desperate act to rid herself of the stigma, and though the punishment for such a calculated crime was death, the court commuted it to transportation.

Elizabeth was not the first and would not be the last Axholme woman to be tried for maternal infanticide. In 1811, Mary Jewitt described as a good-looking, twenty-three-year-old woman from West Stockwith, found herself on trial accused of the willful murder of her illegitimate son. She had an arrangement with a local lady called Martha Ducker who, for a fee set at 4 shillings a week had nursed the child from the age of five weeks. It was an arrangement popularly known as 'baby farming' and served women who had lost all sense of their maternal instincts or could not find a refuge where they could keep the child. One major advantage of this system was that few questions were asked. It assured the mother that her baby would be given the proper care in return for a few shillings a week or 'adopted' for a flat one-time fee. Papers of the day were full of advertisements from people requesting to look after children. There was no formal procedure for adoption in England until 1914 and, while some advertisements were legitimate requests by childless couples, many were from those solely interested in payments that accompanied the children.

It seems after two weeks, Mary found she could not meet the cost and told Martha that her mother, who lived at Saltmarsh, would be taking over the duties of the nurse at a shilling a week less. She had arranged for the two to meet at Crowle, where the child would be handed over. On the morning of the tragedy, Mary called on Martha at 10 o'clock and took the child. At the trial, Martha testified that Mary had always seemed an attentive mother who provided the child with more than enough clothes and seemed 'middling fond of the infant.' She confirmed that the child, 'though small was in good health' when Mary took it away.

On her way to Crowle, Mary called at a public house in Epworth where William Almond, the publican, saw her feed and warm the child. It was a cold day, and she had already walked six or seven miles. Three hours later he saw her return through Epworth, but this time the child was not with her and the speed at which she was walking suggested to him that she could not have got to and back from Crowle in the time.

Several days later, John Unwin from Crowle, was riding along the bank of 'Double River' when his mare reared 'as if being struck.' Looking into the river, John saw something floating and by the extended arm recognised it as an infant. He felt unable to investigate further so rode to the house of John Watson and told him what he had seen. Watson went to the scene, confirmed Unwin's suspicions, and went home to get a basket. The two servants who accompanied him hauled the body out of the water and found it to be a male child, with a 'worsted garter round its neck and a swathe round its legs' – both attached to a large stone.

The authorities placed Mary in Lincoln Castle to await her trial. When questioned, Mary refused to explain the death of the child, so it was left to others to bring forth evidence. Thomas Lightfoot, a surgeon from Crowle, believed the 'prominence of the eyes and a blackness in the face' suggested strangulation. He believed the body had been in the drain for about a week. From the marks on the body he concluded it possibly had 'been destroyed by violence,' but because of the putrid state of the body could not be sure whether a ligature had been placed before or after death. Martha Ducker confirmed that the child wore the same clothes as those when she handed it back to Mary. Summing up, the judge reminded the jury that because of doubts over the state of the child when placed in the river he was not looking for a guilty verdict. After deliberating for half an hour, the jury brought in a verdict of not guilty, but in an intriguing statement suggested the authorities might 'look elsewhere for the perpetrator of the crime.'

Seventy years later, another male child met a similar fate. The mother, Sarah Coakes a twenty-one-year-old single woman of West Butterwick, had been suffering from depression since the birth a week before. There was a history of instability in the family; twelve months earlier Sarah had been in an asylum for some years, and her father was currently serving a six-month period in the asylum at Bracebridge Heath in Lincoln. After her release, Sarah seemed to be more settled and now lived with her grandmother. When the child would not settle to the breast, Sarah asked that she be left alone. Soon after, her grandmother heard the sound of a door closing and when she returned found Sarah had left the room with the baby. As she called out for Sarah, the girl returned empty-handed. When she asked where the baby was, Sarah replied, 'I have thrown it in the Trent.' Afraid that Sarah might attempt suicide the grandmother locked her in the room. Then, after calling to her neighbour for help, both ran to the river bank. They found the child's body floating close to shore and though they managed to recover it they were unable to revive it. When they questioned Sarah, she replied 'I was forced to do it.' At her trial, despite Sarah's background of instability, the jury returned a verdict of 'willful murder.'

The above cases made headlines in provincial papers such as the Stamford Mercury and the Lincolnshire Echo. In July 1861, a crime so horrendous that it reached the national press caused a sensation throughout the Isle. Headlined as 'The Haxey Murders,' the story centred on Ann Wilson, the wife of George Wilson, a respectable farmer from Westwoodside. The couple, who lived in 'comfortable circumstances,' had three children, Lucy aged 3, William aged 4 and Elizabeth aged 8. On the fateful day, George left home to go to Worksop on business. His next call was at his mother's house in Wheatley the day after and upon arriving he was surprised to see his wife waiting for him. When he asked what she had done with the children, she replied that she had taken care of them and they were safe. When he challenged her further, she replied, 'They are safe in heaven.'

It seems that soon after George left, Ann went next door to ask John Webster if she could borrow his pony and cart to meet her husband in Wheatley. Next day Webster went past the Wilson's house, and although the blinds were drawn and the house seemed empty, he saw Ann washing at the sink. Shortly after, she went to Webster's house for the cart and he assumed she would return home to pick up the children. Unknown to him Ann had put the three children in the soft water cistern, the youngest first. The cistern, covered by a huge flat stone slab, contained some five hundred gallons of water to a depth of about two feet. At three o'clock the next day, Webster heard cries of distress coming from the Wilson's house. He found George standing over the cistern, looking down, having removed the stone. Inside Webster saw the leg of the elder girl. Climbing into the tank he found the bodies of the three children 'quite stiff' and still in their nightgowns. He found it hard to comprehend as Anne had always been fond of her children and kind to them.

At her trial, the court heard that Ann, a small woman dressed in

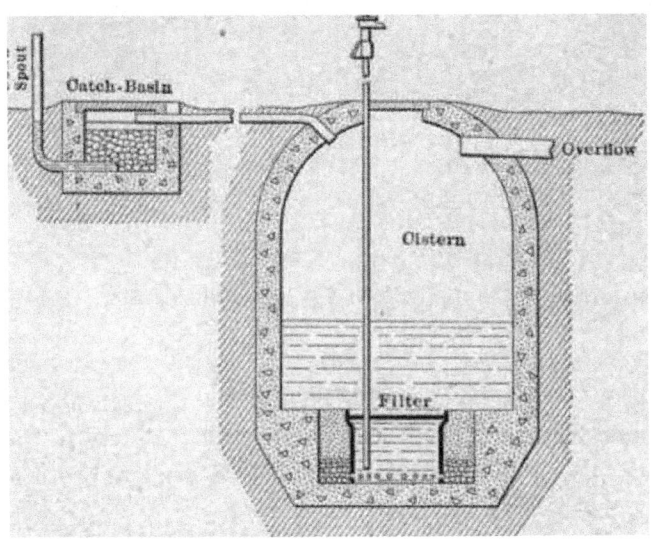

A typical Victorian cistern.

black, had suffered the recent loss of her eighteen-week-old baby. The loss seemed to have affected her mind and she complained of pains in her head. Mary Webster, wife of John, stated she had heard Ann say, 'How much better my children would be if they were in heaven.' At one time she said it would be a good thing if the little boy was in heaven, for 'it would be a bad thing if he grew up to be a drunkard.' In the dock, Ann had to support herself by grasping the rail front of her. It caused a murmur of sympathy throughout the court. When asked how she had committed the crime she claimed she had received help from 'a black man.' She spoke of fetching the youngest first, kissing it all the way down the stairs before pushing into the cistern. She told the court the child 'grabbed hold of a mop and pulled at it' but she forced the child down again. She went on to say, 'I then fetched the middle one, and afterwards the eldest.' Throughout her examination, she seldom moved her head though her eyes moved restlessly over the barrister's table

Several other witnesses spoke of how Ann's demeanour changed after the death of her eighteen-week-old baby. She repeatedly asked her sisters for their blessing, appeared dull and melancholy, spoke of pains in her head and worried about living in 'such a wicked world.' Dr. Pritchard, a surgeon from Stockwith, gave evidence that confirmed Ann was in a poor mental state. He spoke of attending her twice in the past month and thinking she was 'not of sound mind at the time.' He advised her friends to 'let her have cheerful society,' thinking that such a course of action would strengthen her mind.

At this point, the judge intervened to direct the jury to consider the evidence from which he deduced it was apparent the prisoner 'was not in a sane state of mind when she destroyed the children.' He spoke of Ann 'labouring under a kind of religious melancholy, or delusional equivalent' and considering it 'her duty to the Almighty that she should send her children to him and release them from the cares and the troubles which she believed would beset them in this world.' After a brief consultation, the jury acquitted Ann due to her mental state. Thanking the jury for arriving at a just decision, the judge ordered Ann to be detained at her Majesty's pleasure. In

A cistern with the cap removed.

a cutting remark 'The Sporting Chronicle' closed their account of the trial with the words 'There is no doubt she is insane!'

On 29 March 1917 P.C. Hallam received information that a family of gypsies, living in two hooded caravans in fields close to the railway line at Haxey Gate, had buried a newborn child at midnight. Digging into the earth by the side of a dyke on Cornley Lane, just off Tindale Bank in Haxey Parish, Hallam came across the body of a newborn child, wrapped in cloth, two feet down. At his side was Henrietta Smith, one of the family who helped bury the child. She had suffered a crisis of conscience when the two caravans pulled out and left the next day and opted to stay behind; this enabled her to go in secret to the police. She recounted the events as she remembered them; how the party had left the caravan with her expecting them to walk to Haxey churchyard where they would bury the body. Instead, they walked along the lane until one of the men found a suitable spot beside the dyke and began scraping out the soil with his bare hands. As Henrietta stood aside holding the body, the rest joined in digging furiously and furtively to make the hole deep enough. Pushing herself into the hedgerow behind Henrietta became entangled among the twigs and briars that seemed to hold her fast preventing her from moving to place the baby in its shallow grave. Eventually one of the men took the baby from her, and she watched as he placed it in the ground. With little ceremony, they pushed the earth back into place, then stood around holding hands. Apart from Henrietta, no one present shed a tear. On the way back, one of the women put a comforting arm across her shoulders and told her that, although the baby's body was 'lost in the earth, its soul would be in Heaven.'

Later, when the coroner examined the body, he could not determine whether the child had been born dead or 'disposed of' at birth. At the trial in Lincoln Assizes the jury, under direction, found there was no evidence against Hookey Booth and Albert

Margreaves who assisted with the burial, leaving the judge to discharge both men. Having taken no part in the concealment, Henrietta saw the charges against her dropped. Mary Ingram, the mother of the child, was found guilty. As she had spent two and a half months in prison awaiting trial, his lordship thought this to be sufficient punishment and ordered her release.

Finally, in this catalogue of despair, we come to a case that made headlines in 1903 under the caption – 'Sensation at Luddington.' Katie Smith, a local girl, had managed to conceal her pregnancy right up to the last. There were some in the village who claimed to have noticed her debilitating condition but did not link it to her 'being with child' as she had not lived with her husband for some considerable time. She gave birth in the cellar of her house at around midnight in early January, and it was her temporary disappearance that caused some alarm amongst her neighbours. When P.C. Dodson arrived at the house, expecting to undertake a search for a missing person, he found Katie in a distressed state. What led him to suspect foul play is not recorded in the newspaper reports, but upon searching the cellar, he came upon the body of a newborn male child under a pile of rubble. Someone had taken up the bricks in the floor, scraped a shallow grave and placed the bagged-up body in the hole. When superintendent Wilkinson arrived, he cautioned Katie. Initially, she denied all knowledge of the crime saying, 'I don't know anything about it.' Eventually, however, she confessed and went on to say, 'It's no use telling stories about it, the child is mine, but it was dead when it was born.' At her trial a few weeks later, she insisted again that the child had been born dead and not knowing what to do she had buried it, meaning to take it to the churchyard in a box when she felt able to do so. Members of the jury were told the baby boy was plump and well-developed, being 9lbs. in weight and nineteen and a half inches long; there was no evidence of violence on the child. Dr.

Messiter testified that, in his opinion, the child had 'drawn breath but had been neglected since birth.' He estimated the boy had been buried within an hour of birth. He pointed out that he could not be certain, even if the child had received the appropriate care, whether it would have lived.

The evidence was not sufficient to charge Katie with murder. She accepted a charge of concealment of a body which carried a short period of imprisonment. Throughout the ordeal, Katie presented as a frail and confused young lady. The judge considered the time she had been in prison awaiting trial when he sentenced her to three further months imprisonment.

CHAPTER SIXTEEN

Good Cop Bad Cop

MAYHEM

Henry Tooms became police superintendent of the Axholme Division in the 1850s on a salary of £80 per annum – about £9,000 in today's money. With the help of his seven constables, he set about clearing the Isle's streets of vagrants, arresting drunks, detaining farmers who drove their carts in a 'furious manner,' sneaking into public houses in the hope of catching publicans serving customers out of hours and laying in wait for poachers. The more literate frequently complained, through letters to the newspapers, of the loss of privacy and freedom caused by policemen who seemed to everywhere, watching everything. Seen by many as an excellent officer, it seems Tooms had almost as much trouble from his constables as he did from the locals. One, P.C. James Stothard, received a month's imprisonment for a 'violation of duty' when accompanying a female prisoner to gaol and another, P.C. John Favell was dismissed for being drunk and incapable when on duty at Epworth's Martinmas Market.

When Tooms disappeared suddenly on 21 October 1861, allegations began to circulate that he was suspected of embezzling money. Many locals refused to believe it but five days later, after being found and arrested when walking in front of the Elephant and Castle public house in Newington, London, Superintendent Thoresby of the Horncastle Division brought him back to Epworth to face charges. Stood before a packed court at Epworth, he was charged with forging his expenses and committed for trial at Lincoln's Winter Assizes.

The first charge he faced was that of forging two receipts for services rendered by Doctor Bennett. The good doctor denied ever producing such receipts stating that they were not in his handwriting. The court read out three further charges: one of forging receipts from Mr. Wilkinson (chemist), a second of forging receipts from Mr. Alfred Trousdall (surgeon) and the third for claiming to have received 7s 6d for coal he never ordered. Full of remorse, Tooms pleaded guilty, but in his defence, he claimed he had fallen foul of the county's impossible accounting procedures. To those familiar with the scheme it was not an unreasonable claim as the payments system was exceedingly complex but the court's decision rested on the fact that he had used the confusion in the system to hide his embezzlement. The crime of forgery carried the death penalty but, perhaps because of his previous record of bringing criminals to justice, the judge ordered Tooms to serve ten years penal servitude. His time in prison left him a broken man, but his misdemeanour did commit the police authority to overhauling the accounting system radically.

Epworth police station and courthouse. From a drawing by Sid Sedgwick.

It seems the system was not overhauled radically enough, however, because some fifty years later another Police Superintendent left his post under similar circumstances. Superintendent Hill seems to have developed a system of taking in money in fines and costs but issuing receipts at a lower figure. When this scam came to light, magistrates summoned him to appear at court in Epworth. The bench heard evidence that on one occasion he asked a youth named Albert Lindley, working as a groom for Messrs. Camp Brothers, who supplied traps for the police, to make out a bill for 15/- for work amounting to 7/-. Somewhat in awe of Hill's position, Lindley did as instructed. On another occasion, Hill charged for clothing two Norwegians, Hugus Hanain and Karl Oken who had deserted their ship in Goole. They never received the clothing. The magistrates concluded that these, and other charges against Hill, were more serious than they would have been if brought against an 'ordinary individual.' They concluded that those concerned had been so under the control of Hill that they felt they had no power to resist someone in such a position of authority. Hill pleaded guilty to the charges, knowing that in doing so he would be dismissed from the force and relinquish the superannuated allowance he'd built up over the past twenty-five years. He was, in effect, a ruined man and stood before the court sorry and ashamed. His wife and three daughters resolved to stand by him and hoped he would be given the chance to make a new start, possibly in another country. Hill had used the money to help fuel his drink problem, the outcome he maintained of serving the public in a demanding and under-appreciated capacity. The hours were long, there were few rest days, and an ever-present danger of assault or injury saw many like Hill turn to drink as a means of release from the strains of the job.

One night in late 1916, shouts of 'Murder' and 'German Spy' rent the night air in Crowle. The events that followed began in terror, moved on to panic and ended in high farce. Apparently, a man from Grimsby, seeking to hire a taxi from Charles Hill at the White Hart, found his request denied. To Charles, there was something suspicious about the man's demeanour and his explanation that he wanted to meet someone, somewhere between Frodingham and Winterton seemed deliberately vague and imprecise.*

When Charles declared he would not accept the fare, the man struck him across the face with a cane, breaking it in two. He then raced out of the yard threatening to shoot anyone who attempted to stop him. Charles, along with others alerted by the noise from the altercation, gave chase and cornered the man in Cockin's Wood on Wharf Road. Challenged again, this time by Mr. W. F. Clarke, the man repeated his threat and warned Clarke he would 'blow his brains out if he came any closer.' Undeterred, Clarke rushed him and a violent struggle ensued. Overpowered by weight of numbers, the posse bundled the man into the very taxi he had been denied access to only a few minutes earlier. By the time the taxi arrived at the police station news had spread through the town and a large crowd gathered outside. As the taxi drew up, their eagerness to help overcame caution and they surged forward, manhandling one of the occupants into the building in a 'disordered and chaotic manner.' Inside, this confusion and disarray continued, with everyone keen to bring the prisoner to justice. When the police turned a light on the offender's face, however, it became apparent they had seized the wrong man – somewhat amusingly it transpired the crowd had 'arrested' the parish councillor who, when released, was left 'gasping for breath and rubbing ruefully various parts of his anatomy!' The architect of the affray, a Mr. Herbert Lewis, remained locked in the taxi in the safe custody of Mr. Clarke. It transpired later that Mr. Lewis had returned from active service

*Taken from reports in The Epworth Bells, The Crowle Advertiser and The Yorkshire Evening Standard

recently having been taken ill and was suffering from delusions following a nervous breakdown. Nowadays his reaction would be attributed to 'Combat Stress' – the most common symptoms being fatigue, slower reaction times, indecision, disconnection from one's surroundings, and an inability to prioritise. As things began to calm down, the police fined Lewis ten shillings for assaulting the taxi driver and then decided to transport him back to Grimsby and leave it to the authorities there to determine what to do with him.

In the late 1890s at the close of the potato harvest, what were termed 'dangerous characters' were seen loitering about Keadby. One night, about twenty of them 'invaded' the Mariners' Arms. They put the landlord and landlady to flight by making threats of violence, and at once 'proceeded to partake freely of the contents of the beer cellar.' Unfortunately, the only police constable the village possessed was away, and the marauders helped themselves to half an hour's unlimited drinking. Their shouts of revelry, however, soon turned to cursing and brawling and it was at this juncture that P.C. Bursnall, known in the district as 'a smart, burly constable,' arrived on the scene. He rushed in amongst the party and collared them one after another by the neck and 'other portions of their attire,' and hurled them over a nearby fence. The din and the language were indescribable. One big, hulking fellow lunged at the constable and tried to slash his face with a heavy belt and buckle, kicking out furiously, but the officer stepped aside deftly and caught him on the jaw with a stinging left-hander. The man was unconscious before he hit the ground. After clearing the premises, the men organised themselves outside pub, and lay in wait for the constable to emerge. As he left, the gang fell upon him, and a tussle ensued. At one point Burnsall was almost pitched into the River Trent. However, he fought back desperately and managed to secure two of his assailants. As help arrived, the rest of ruffians dispersed, and the much bruised and battered constable set off with his prisoners to Epworth Police station. Newspaper reports from the time talk of there 'never having been such an occurrence in the history of Keadby.'

It seems P.C. Bursnall took the incident very much in his stride. When the two men appeared before the magistrates and received seven days hard labour for drunken affray, 'the gallant officer' spoke up for the one who had attempted to kick him saying: 'I'd rather he wasn't charged with assault, sir, if you don't mind; he has not had it all his own way.' He reported that he was on duty in Crowle when he received the call about the disturbances in Keadby. Arriving there at about six o'clock he said that he had been 'kept busy until about ten o'clock protecting the publicans from being assaulted.' The following night he attended again and spent a couple of hours ejecting drunks first from one public house then another. When asked if he required additional help his modest reply was that he was confident he could 'take care of himself.' The report of the affray in the Sheffield Telegraph concluded by stating that P.C. Bursnall 'is certainly one of the smartest men in the Lincolnshire Force and is possessed of considerable courage and determination.'

Ten years later, on 10 June 1866, Acting Sergeant Summers and P.C. John Waddingham, responding to information received, were searching the roads around Crowle for a 'notorious poacher,' sixty-three-tear-old Willy Quickfall. Described as a very determined individual, characterised by a love of adventure, he was often the worse for drink. Spotting him further up 'the high road' on the Lazenby estates, the two policemen closed in on him. The wily poacher, seeing Waddingham, the younger (and perhaps fitter) of the two policemen approaching, set off across the fields. Three-quarters of a mile later and with Waddingham almost upon him, Quickfall, hampered by a drain turned to face the constable and raised his gun. True to his boast that he would never be captured Quickfall warned Waddingham not to come any closer. Putting duty before discretion, Waddingham moved forward to effect an arrest. Quickfall discharged one of the barrels of his shotgun and, in the words of the newspaper report, 'awfully shattered his pursuer's left arm.' Calmly replacing the spent cartridge, he stood over the injured man. For several seconds the pair stared at one another in silence; Quickfall holding the policeman's gaze over the sights of his gun, and Waddingham clutching his limp and blood-soaked arm. It was Willy Quickfall who broke the standoff when, turning on his heel, he beat a hasty retreat.

Waddingham staggered back to where his sergeant waited but collapsed from loss of blood before he reached him. Once found, Sergeant Summers arranged for him to be conveyed to the doctor in Crowle. Initially, there seemed hope that the pellets could be removed from the policeman's shoulder but this proved beyond the skill of the medical profession. The surgical team determined upon amputation as the only course of action and two day's later, after a strong dose of chloroform they removed the arm. According to reports from the time, Waddingham suffered intense pain during the procedure as the chloroform 'had but little effect upon him.' At first, his recovery seemed doubtful, but his condition improved gradually. The injury ended a promising career.

As Quickfall was well-known throughout the district, expectations were high that he would be caught, especially as Captain Bicknall published a reward of £50 for information leading to his arrest. After an extensive manhunt, Quickfall finally ended up in custody after going to his brother-in-law's house. Tried at Lincoln Assizes, initially on a charge of attempted murder, he was eventually found guilty of the lesser charge of causing grievous bodily harm. For this, the judge sentenced him to five years penal servitude. He served his time at the prison on Dartmoor. The police force dismissed Summers from the local constabulary for cowardice.

When P.C. Dean of Crowle set off down the road from Crowle to Eastoft on his beat he noticed the gate that led into a grass field was partially open. He thought little of it until a few yards further on he heard noises coming from behind the hedge. Turning back he went through the gate into the field he came upon nineteen-year-old George Thomas Sharpe, a sack maker, and Thomas Cunningham (25), a local hawker, both carrying guns. Sharpe had a standard sized shotgun but Cunningham's had been shortened. When Dean asked what business they had in the field, Cunningham swore, raised his gun, pointed at the constable's head and discharged it. Several pellets hit Dean behind the right ear as he turned his head away; the impact causing him to fall into the hedge. As he staggered to his feet, Cunningham asked Sharpe to give him his gun so he could 'give the bastard some more.' Sharpe hesitated which allowed Dean time to turn and stumble away. Although Cunningham set off in pursuit there were no more shots fired.

Constable Dean made his way to Crowle Police Station where Mr. Ellis, the surgeon, dressed the wound that, by now, was bleeding profusely. Although the jagged wound was not deep, parts of Dean's skull were exposed, and the surgeon declared it 'dangerous.' It would have been worse had his helmet not taken much of the impact. William Taylor, the inspector of police, set off for the house where Cunningham lived but could not find him. Going next door, he looked in George Quickfall's coal-hovel and found the long-barrelled gun. Later, he went to Sharpe's mother's house and found the sawn-off shotgun in the bedroom.

The police caught up with Cunningham in Derbyshire and brought him back to Epworth for trial. His immediate response was to call Dean a 'liar.' He then went on to say it was the first time he had been locked up for poaching and he would 'bet his life it would be the last.' The prosecutor, Mr. Attenborough, asked the jury to consider that, if the shot had been delivered straight instead of sideways, then the consequence could have been fatal. He informed them that Cunningham had been in court twice before, once for assault and robbery and the second time for assaulting a police officer. For this, he had been imprisoned for twelve calendar months. He asked the jury to consider a sentence of no less than seven years. Cunningham's defence counsel asked the jury to consider the fact that no one in Crowle or the surrounding area had reported hearing the discharge of a gun. He also questioned why no pellets were taken from the wound to Dean's ear, contending that the wound was caused by the but of the gun – there had been no attempt to murder the constable so the jury should only consider a charge of wounding. He tried to bring the evidence of the constable into disrepute by claiming that, in the darkness, he could not be sure which of the two men had fired the shot. It did not impress the jury as they found Cunningham guilty. Considering his previous record, and as a warning to others, the judge sentenced him to seven years' penal servitude.

CHAPTER SEVENTEEN

Threats to Health and a Close Shave

MISADVENTURE

Until the 1930s, the settlements of Axholme had no system of sewers or water pipes. From medieval times, garbage and human waste, thrown into the streets, flowed along channels in the open road. On days when there was no rain to flush away the refuse, the aroma became quite off-putting. It prompted one Epworth resident to write, 'all the sewage runs on top of the streets and on the side of the pavements - soap, matter from fold yards, in fact, everything that is liquid.' Refuse thrown down in the Market Place 'floated' the length of the town in an open gutter, terminating in an unenclosed cesspool down West End. The system survived in part as medical advice at the time continued to embrace the mantra that 'what is offensive to the nose is not always ruinous to health.'

Rats, lice and fleas flourished in the rush-strewn floors of wood framed houses. This 'livestock' mingled in the spittle, vomit, dog (and human) urine and the remnants of meals, creating an indescribable filth. In this putrefying mess, human parasites thrived and diseases like tuberculosis, 'sweating' sickness, smallpox, influenza, mumps and gastrointestinal infections festered. Things were little better outside. Here, manure from cows and other animals collected in farmyards along the highway. In wet weather, the runoff found its way into homes and led to typhoid and dysentery. Allied to severe winters, suffocating mists and crop failure, medieval Axholme was not a healthy place to live. In the nine months between August 1590 and April 1591, records show that one-hundred and thirty-eight people died from malnutrition and disease in Haxey alone.

Things reached such a state that Axholme landowners opted for a system termed 'early inheritance,' whereby they assigned their legacy to their children at the earliest opportunity (even if this meant placing their lands in trust to their wife until the child reached twenty-one).

Of course, in common with medical ignorance of the time, what doctors in the Isle lacked was any concept of viruses or bacteria. Given this lack of understanding, they and their contemporaries reasoned it was a person's behaviour that brought on illness. An unhealthy body was an imbalance of the body's humours, and their role was to help redress this inequality. They carried out the harmful practice of bloodletting; their main 'tool' being the leech, something which the freshwaters of Axholme provided in abundance. To alleviate their aches and pains, many an Isle household drank tea, brewed from the seeds and pods of the opium poppy. This potion gave them a warming, somewhat euphoric sensation throughout the body. For many, however, there followed nausea, drowsiness, severe constipation and in several cases early death.

A hundred years later, the death rate in Haxey over a similar winter period, had dropped to ninety-one. By now people realised that the room next to a privy was an unhealthy place in which to live, and across the Isle 'gongfermers' were abroad to clear out the cesspits. It wasn't until the nineteenth century, however, that the importance of hygiene was recognised. When the authorities began collection data, they were horrified by the incidence of infant mortality. Whooping cough, acute diseases of the lungs and diarrhoea accounted for almost fifty per cent of Axholme deaths in the under fives. In the wider population twenty-five per cent of deaths were due to phthysis or consumption; thirteen per cent from bronchitis and nine from heart attack.

A look at the census details from 1841 to 1901 shows some Victorian families where the woman was almost continually pregnant, between marriage and menopause. Childbirth was risky and painful and surviving infanthood a constant battle. In his annual medical return for 1899, Dr. Messiter reported the mortality rate for children under five (excluding those whose short lives were ended by infanticide) accounted for 31% of all deaths.

By 1911, the total number of deaths in Epworth fell from a high of 110 to 65. Deaths from smallpox and measles had all but been eradicated, and outbreaks of scarlet fever were on the wane. Deaths from diarrhoea, however, remained at worrying levels. The improving situation prompted Alderman Blaydes to reference Epworth as one of the 'healthiest towns in England,' with the lowest death rate in the county of Lincolnshire. To back up this assertion, he referred to figures showing 152 residents of Epworth surpassing the age of seventy years, twenty of whom were over eighty (the oldest being Mrs. Joseph Boyes aged 93).

From March 1918 through to late 1919, Britain had been fighting a deadly influenza pandemic. In late 1918 the deaths column of the Epworth Bells had recorded over 60 deaths for November and early December alone. Schools closed for weeks at a time, and when they reopened, many had to close again, as the incidents of infection increased. Church congregations dwindled as people shunned close contact. Other places where the public gathered, such as picture houses, initiated voluntary closures. It left a population, weakened by four years of privation, struggling to fight the effects of infection. In a very short time, from Westwoodside to Garthorpe and from Keadby to Pelfintax the influenza epidemic took a heavy toll on every parish. Public health departments implemented greater restrictive measures than those imposed during the war, and a nation that had accepted these restrictions on freedom had to commit further to putting the requirements of all ahead of personal need. Soldiers, weakened by malnourishment, the stresses of combat and by chemical attacks, found their immune system more susceptible to attack from this virus. Those bound by the continuing privations of close quarter living found themselves at even greater risk. Sergeant Joseph Roberts of Misterton was working for the Military Police processing men in the Etaples area when the 'flu epidemic struck and spread quickly. He caught the disease, died on 27 November and was buried in Etaples Military Cemetery.

The scourge of this epidemic (some called it 'Spanish Lady') hit the community of West Butterwick hard, and the Pilsworth family suffered greatly. The first to be struck down was Thomas Ellis Pilsworth (25), and his death was followed quickly by that of his wife, Alice. (27). The next to suffer was his father, Watson, aged 63, followed by the death of his daughter, Miriam, aged 22. Their funerals took place over six days. Their eldest son, George, had been killed in action in France on 19 September 1918. The family were active members of the Primitive Methodist Church where Watson had taken on the role of Sunday school teacher, and it was here the remaining members of the family sought compassion and support. Those bearing the coffins included fellow employees of Messrs. Dennis and Godfrey and neighbours, with a number of scholars from the Primitive Sunday School among the mourners. All in the village described the sadness as 'overwhelming.' In Haxey, the town doctor was one of the first to catch the disease and, though he sought to work through it and administer to his patients, the effort proved too much. The town was fortunate that two nurses arrived from Gainsborough to take on the doctor's workload. One of them, Nurse Graveson, who worked by day, paid four hundred home visits in six days, on occasions travelling from one side of the town to the other several times each day. Nurse Spacie worked through the night among the most severe cases. She, too, contracted the disease, as did a relief doctor sent in her stead.

Members of the clergy found themselves overwhelmed, comforting the sick and undertaking the many funerals. The vicar of Haxey, himself a victim, appealed to the Bishop of Lincoln for support but, with so many clergy ill across the county, there was no one available. The advice he received was to close the church to Sunday services to reduce the spread of the disease.

Among those who died were: Mr. T. G. Harris (Chairman of the Parish Council) and his wife; Mrs. Cooper, a staunch supporter of the church even through long ill health; Miss R. English, the doctor's youngest daughter; brothers Morley and Frank Whitehead; Mr. Hill, who lived long enough to welcome his son back from the front; Mrs. A. Burrell; Mrs Turnbull, recently married; Mr. Wrigley, his daughter and a grandchild; Mr. Holgate from the Carr; John and George Catley, Jacob Fox and sixteen year old G. Steadman. It was not until Christmas 1919 that Dr. Messiter felt able to record a let up in the epidemic.

When George Marshall, a labourer from Crowle, called in at Harold Goodison's barber's shop on 29 November 1913, he was looking forward to an invigorating shave. He was not, by any means, a regular customer but did drop by occasionally for a shave. Unfortunately, at some point, Goodison's blade nicked Marshall's skin beneath his chin. It was a simple mistake and both men resolved the incident amicably, although Goodison did not apply any disinfectant to the cut. Two days later, however, Marshall developed a rash around the cut which resulted in his face swelling. He mentioned the matter to Goodison who said he should call again and they would 'come to some terms.' Although he called again later, he found that Goodison avoided him, so he went to the doctor who diagnosed his condition as barber's rash and Erysipelas, an acute infection of the upper dermis. He signed Marshall off work for eight weeks.

Described as a 'curious case' when it came before Thorne County Court, George Marshall sought damages of £46/10/- for negligence in shaving, stating he was only earning 18/- a week, as against his previous wage of 30/-. He claimed that Goodison did not change the water he used to shave him or the towel he had used on previous customers. Marshall claimed further that this was not the only case of the kind that had happened at this shop. Goodison defended his actions by telling the court he always had an urn of boiling water to hand and used fresh water for each customer. He said he always rinsed his brush and dipped the razor in boiling water each time. After shaving, he sponged the customer down and used an antiseptic spray. Marshall, he said, had stopped him on Christmas Eve and asked him for compensation. He had told him that he would have to prove he got the rash at his shop before he could do anything.

Witnesses called before the judge all supported Goodison's claims of running a clean shop. Charles Fox declared that if the shop was not hygienic, he would have ceased to be a customer a long time ago. Arthur Storey agreed and stated that he attended four times a week, but it was Austin Briggs, a daily customer, whose supportive evidence carried the greatest weight. Marshall's inflated claim fell apart when under oath, he revealed he was not in employment at the time of the incident. Summing up, the judge ruled that Marshall could not expect any recompense for lost wages. He upheld Marshall's claim that he had caught a barber's rash at the defendant's shop but did not consider it brought on the Erysipelas. He awarded Marshall £5 and costs.

CHAPTER EIGHTEEN

A Novel Mystery

MYSTERY

In April 1903, John Lane, founder and publisher at Bodley Head in Virgo Street, London received a parcel enclosed in a red box. When he opened the box, he found inside the manuscript of a novel. The novel had no title, no ascribed author and no accompanying letter. He sent the book to the company's reader who wrote a favourable review. Lane read it himself and found it met his passion for audacious, contemporary fiction. He likened it to the historical romances of writers such as Robert Louis Stevenson and Walter Scott. Eager to find the author and no doubt with an eye to financial gain, Lane placed the following advertisement in the press:

TO AUTHORS

NOTICE – If the writer of an historical novel without a title, Author's name or address, sent some weeks ago to The Bodley Head in a Red Box, will communicate with the publisher, he will hear something to his advantage.

– John Lane, Virgo Street, London, W.2

It was a tempting advert and it had the desired effect. There was, what one newspaper called, 'a hullabaloo of excitement,' but no viable author came forward. Lane tried again, going further by stating he would 'publish the book at a certain date unless the author came forward.'

John Lane was as good as his word and published the book, giving it the only title he could think of – 'The Manuscript in a

Red Box.' The name stuck and all the controversy surrounding it ensured there was interest from the start. The book told the tale of the haughty and self-reliant residents of the Isle of Axholme and their struggles with the Dutch drainers who came to the region to change the landscape forever. The story had all the elements of a nineteenth-century romantic thriller – a twisting storyline with an engrossing plot, lively characters, an eerie backdrop in isolated surroundings and a romance to rival that of a modern-day Romeo and Juliet. It received critical acclaim as readers sought to identify with the Isle's trackless, historical setting that was credible yet obscure.

When the book came out, John Lane received a flood of letters from people claiming to be the author. Some he eliminated immediately, others proved more tricky, but none convinced him of their suitability. The author was clearly an accomplished writer and someone who knew the Isle and its antiquity very well. Although never proved conclusively at the time, later reprints of the

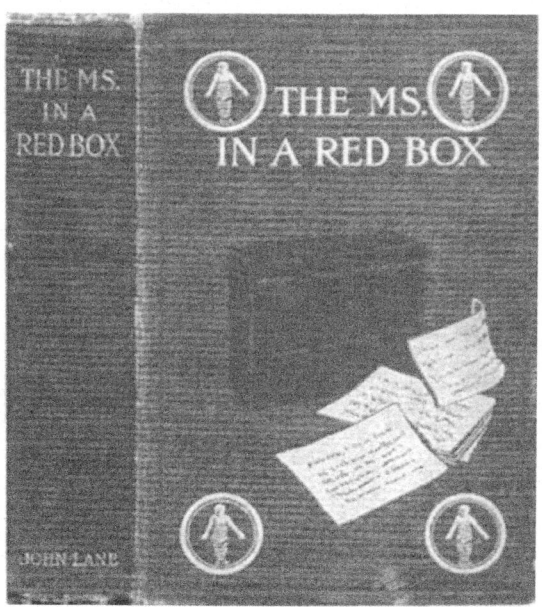

A first edition Manuscript in a Red Box.

book, following an interview with the Epworth Bells, credited the author as John Arthur Hamilton, born in Staffordshire in 1854 and a Congregational Minister at Crowle from 1870-1878. It was his first pastorate; he went on to hold office in Saltaire and Penzance, where he named his Cornish home 'Axholme.' From the opening lines of the book, we see Hamilton exerting his knowledge of the geographical context of the area. His wife came from an Axholme family, and it was there where his children were born. His introduction begins with a simple statement: 'On the tenth of May in the year sixteen hundred and twenty-seven, I rode from Temple Belwood to Crowle....' He described himself as 'nearly an Islonian as a man can be who was not born there.' It seems his time in Axholme stayed fresh in his memory throughout the rest of his life. The Manuscript in a Red Box was his first published story but not his first book as he had previously written a volume of parables especially for children entitled 'The Mountain Path.' He is credited with pioneering the idea of using stories for children in his sermons to give them a deeper insight into religious texts.

The principal theme of the book is the romance between a Commoner, Frank Vavasour of Temple Belwood whose family tried to stop the drainage, and Anna Goel, daughter of a Dutch Participant. Hamilton adds kidnap and torture to the mix through the dastardly Lord Sheffield, a love rival of Vavasour, who rules the Isle of Axholme from the family seat at Mulgrave Castle, West Butterwick where there are rumours of torture and false imprisonment. And it is this that leads to the book's second mystery; how could someone so encompassed by religious zeal be the author of such a strange book that hints at bizarre visions and impiety? Perhaps it was this dichotomy that initially saw Hamilton seek anonymity. Finally, the third mystery centres on suggestions at the time and right up to the present day that Lane and Hamilton collaborated in a sophisticated deception, designed to create 'an enigmatic significance' to the book and thereby advance its salability.

Hamilton's other book, Captain John Lister, focuses on events during the English Civil War. The hero captain, with his 'dark manly face and lithe, active limbs,' is a Parliamentarian through and through. Sent to the Isle to keep order between the marsh dwellers and the newcomers, the book chronicles the escapades of Lister and his bride to be, the beautiful and mildly Royalist, Mistress Eleanor. There are some who believe that, though the story is a conscientious attempt to recreate the essence of the time, it lacks the excitement of 'Red Box' and its chime is little more than adequate.

CHAPTER NINETEEN

One War after Another

MAYHEM AND MURDER

As the First World War drew to a close, Mr. and Mrs. Frederick Walker of Eastoft Road, Crowle, had cause to regret the late summer. On 28 August 1918, they received news that their nineteen-year-old son, Fred, had been killed in action. Employed on the Great Central Railway before the war, Fred's practical skills had been much sought after and this delayed his entry into the war. He would not arrive in France to join the 1st Battalion, The Sherwood Foresters until April 1918. On the morning of 28 August, the Battalion was strengthening the line when the enemy began firing their artillery into the Foresters' trenches. The intense barrage lasted until 1.50 p.m. and when it lifted the enemy advanced rapidly. Trench raiding and hand-to-hand fighting ensued before the Foresters, using revolvers, rifle butts and bayonets, drove back the enemy attack. Battalion losses amounted to three officers and twenty-one non-commissioned officers killed, fifty-eight men wounded and four missing. After the engagement, Major-General Heneker wrote to the Foresters' commanding officer to say, 'I wish you would convey to all officers and men who were in the line when the Boche attacked you so heavily on the 28th inst., my thanks for the gallant fight they put up. I can always rely on the 1st. Sherwood Foresters to do the right thing. Tell your fellows what I say.' Fred was not alive to hear the acclaim. His 'Statement of Service Form' reads, 'Killed in Action, Place not stated.' On 30 September 1919, however, French authorities identified Fred's body by his disc and buried him at Orchard Dump Cemetery.

His mother requested the words, 'God Rest His Soul - R.I.P' be added to his Commonwealth War Grave headstone. When the army returned Fred's effects to his father in January 1919, they included his disc, letters, photos, his pocketbook, a religious book and a postcard.

Two weeks later the family received the shattering news that their twenty-one-year-old son, Bernard, had also been killed. He was in a cyclist battalion and, as such, rarely committed to action as these units were generally found to be ineffective in combat conditions. In 1918, however, with the deadlock of the trenches over, cyclists proved invaluable for reconnaissance. On 16 September 1918, Bernard was not in combat but repairing a trench when a shell landed where he was working. Of the ten men in his party two men escaped uninjured, three suffered wounds, and the other five died. Bernard was one of these. His commanding officer wrote to Bernard's parents saying that death was instantaneous and 'his loss will be deeply felt throughout the regiment.' Bert Cranidge wrote to say his brother Charles carried Bernard's body to the ambulance and assured his parents 'he suffered no pain and would not know when his time came.' He went on, 'don't grieve too deeply but think of Bernard as he was - one who did his duty to the last with a brave heart.' The authorities buried Bernard in Hagle Dump Cemetery five miles west of Ypres. Thankfully, the Walker's other son, Tom, survived the war.

Not the last soldier from Axholme to die during hostilities but, one of the most poignant deaths was that of Sergeant Leonard Walton of Crowle. Leonard was a reservist and was looking forward to marrying his fiancee, Emma Troope. However, on 5 August 1914, before the marriage could take place, he was ordered abroad. After marching into Belgium, he fought at the Battle of Mons and the subsequent retreat, and the Battles of the Aisne and Marne. Except for a short period of leave and, on one occasion being invalided home with bullet wounds from a Maxim machine gun, he served in frontline duties throughout the war and saw 'much severe fighting.' For him, it had been 'a long war' of danger and privation. For a time he had lived on 'berries and turnips' but always remained alert and willing. His conduct under fire resulted in three battlefield promotions. The sad news of his death came as a further blow to the Walton family. In October 1914 their son, Percy had become the first Crowle soldier to die, although news of his death had not reached his parents until December. Another son, George, posted as missing, eventually turned up safe while their fourth son, Bert, was discharged from the army, a result of serious wounds received in action.

The residents of the Isle received news of the Armistice at 11 o'clock and celebrated by flying flags and ringing church bells. In Crowle, the event generated 'feelings of great thankfulness and enthusiasm.' There was a 'liberal display' of flags; work was temporarily suspended; self-suppression was relaxed and raucous singing, and handshaking became the norm. However, the news brought no joy to Mr. and Mrs. Woodhouse of The Hollies. Three hours earlier they had received a telegram informing them of the death of their son, Henry, a Second Lieutenant in the Duke of Wellington's (West Riding) Regiment. His death at dawn on 4 November, happened when his regiment accompanied 17 British and 11 French divisions in an attack that became known as the Battle of Sambre. Henry's Battalion was one of three West Riding Battalions tasked with capturing the village of Futoy. Thirteen officers and 226 other ranks died in this action. One of those officers was Henry. A party of men from the 9th buried their 2nd lieutenant in a battlefield grave close to where he fell. Following the Armistice, his body was exhumed and reburied in Romeries Communal Cemetery Extension. Henry's father requested the words 'Dearly Loved' should be engraved on his headstone.

In most villages of the Isle, several families mourned the death of two sons, and the family numbers grow if we include brothers-in-law and cousins in the statistics. However, no family gave or lost more, than the Stephenson family of Lansdowne House, Althorpe, and the Dale family of Crowle. James Stephenson, the head of the family and a Lincolnshire Alderman, was a staunch supporter of the war locally and threw himself into the work of the Voluntary Training Corps. He became the chairman of countless committees and ruled on Axholme Tribunal cases. Too old himself to serve, James stood proudly behind his nine children who all contributed to the war effort. In June 1915 he and his wife received the sad news of the death of their thirty-three-year-old son, George. An excellent sportsman and a strong swimmer George had used this skill to save a person from drowning. Accompanying a party of bomb throwers, a skill at which he was quite adept, George (whose battalion nickname was 'Steve') fell to a sniper's bullet. Men from his battalion buried him in a soldier's battlefield grave with full military honours.

In March 1916, James was about to preside over a tribunal hearing when he heard of the death of his son Eric. The tribunal committee was astounded when he turned up at the meeting to fulfil his role. Mr. J. J. Cranidge insisted on chairing the meeting and accepted a proposal for a vote of sympathy for the Alderman and his family. The vote passed in silence. Alderman Stephenson expressed his thanks but insisted on business as usual; he would play an active role in the proceedings. When the tribunal began a farmer from Wroot appeared before the committee to seek an exemption for his sons, 'because they wouldn't be able to stand life in the army,' James Stephenson was in no mood for compromise and gave him short shrift. Equally, when a thirty-three-year-old Garthorpe farmer applied for an exemption for himself and his three labourers, James found it astounding that there should be four men of military age on a farm of moderate size! When the applicant responded that he could not get anyone to fill their places, it was Alderman Stephenson who retorted, 'I am afraid you will have to!'

Eric Stephenson was a second lieutenant in the 4th Battalion, The Lincolnshire Regiment. He was twenty-three-years-old and had been in the trenches for about a week when, like his brother, he too was hit by a sniper's bullet. His captain said of him that he was, 'exceedingly keen in his work and never expected his men to go through any fatigue that he could not do himself.'

In March 1918, the Stephenson family would hear of the death of their youngest son, twenty-one-year-old Urban, a Lieutenant in the 1st Battalion, The Lincolnshire Regiment. A memorial to the three Stephenson boys takes the form of a single-light stained-glass window in Althorpe Memorial Hall. Their mother organised its erection. Across the road, in a corner of Althorpe Churchyard, are their names on a white marble cross.

George, Robert and Tom Dale were sons of Thomas and Evelina Dale of Moorgate Villa, Crowle. At 7.30 a.m. on 1 July 1916, the 8th York & Lancasters went into action on the first day of the Somme. About seventy men got to the third line of the enemy's trenches; the rest were caught up in the ferocious fighting of the first line. The 8th Battalion's casualties were some of the highest suffered on that day. Out of the 680 men and 23 officers who left their trench that morning only 68 returned. George was not among the few who came back.

Robert the youngest enlisted in the army in 1907 and during a period of duty in India contracted a serious but undiagnosed illness. He recovered sufficiently to retrain and entered the Great War in November 1914. In August 1916 Robert was in Salonica when he became ill with malaria. With little hope of recovery, he died on 11 October from dysentery.

Tom enlisted in the Lincolnshire Regiment in the autumn of

1916 but later, he transferred to the Wiltshire Regiment. He was with them on 9 April 1917 when they were tasked with advancing on the Hindenberg Line and became one of the regiments 380 casualties. His body lies in Neuville-Vitasse Road Cemetery. Three sons lost in the space of ten months – a crushing blow to the family.

Willie Chafer celebrated on a Wills' cigarette card.

From towns and villages across the Isle, several men won medals for valour, the most common one being the Military Medal. At least twelve soldiers from Crowle would receive this award. Two Axholme soldiers, however, received a nation's highest honour. On 3 June 1916, Private Willie Chafer recovered a note from a dying messenger and under intense fire set off to deliver it himself. Running along the parapet, in full view of the enemy, he received several gunshot wounds but managed to get the message through. A bullet wound to his left leg, however, proved to be beyond repair and some hours later army surgeons resorted to amputation. Willie received the Victoria Cross at Buckingham Palace on 4 November 1916.

The second soldier was Private Albert Hirst of Epworth. He enlisted in the 15th Battalion, The Prince of Wales' Own, West Yorkshire Regiment (The Leeds Pals) in May 1915 and because of his agility and speed the army assigned him to the role of dispatch runner. Under constant risk of wounding or death, it could take a runner hours to deliver a message over a few hundred metres. Albert spent much of his war in the area around Arras and on many occasions worked for the French command. It was on one such assignment that he received a mortal wound and died on 13 May 1917. His work for the French Army led to the award of the Croix de Guerre – France's highest award for bravery.

Albert Hirst.

Over three hundred soldiers from the Isle died as a result of the war. Several came back with life-changing injuries, including many who suffered the much-misunderstood symptoms of post-traumatic stress disorder. One who counted himself lucky to survive was William Henry Pilsworth. He had endured two and a half years in France though not without incident. Wounded in the leg by a piece of shrapnel and gassed, he felt fortunate to be able to return to his previous occupation at Frodingham steelworks. Three weeks into his job he, his younger brother and another labourer, left their cabin at seven minutes to twelve to reach their place of work on the site. They walked in single file, taking a well-walked shortcut. Along the footpath, steam from the boiler of a crane obscured their vision. Temporarily confused, William walked into the path of another, more active, crane and sustained such terrible injuries that he died within seconds. The coroner recorded a verdict of 'accidental death' and went on to state that there was no need for the men to take the path they did as they could have walked the safe route through the steel mill.

The Second World War brought far less pain to Axholme. There were fewer soldiers' deaths (about 70), most households had more 'creature comforts,' and even though the nation came close to defeat on more than one occasion, many maintained an unbroken optimism that right would triumph over might. There were some who, when looking back, saw the period of the war as the best years of their lives. For the ladies of Axholme, there were dashing Polish airmen at nearby RAF Lindholme, dances and socials at a local hall and the emancipating freedom of taking on roles previously the domain of their menfolk. For the men who did not enlist there was the Home Guard, The Royal Observer Corps, The Civil Defence and a myriad of other organisations where they could play their part in 'keeping the home fires burning.'

Although there were less Axholme casualties and less returning soldiers, those who came back had equally compelling stories to tell. At the outbreak of war, Sid Sedgwick worked as a mechanic and lived at 17 Low Street, Haxey. He joined the Territorial Army at the age of 19 and entered the hostilities as a sapper in the Royal Engineers. Taken prisoner in Tobruk on 21 June 1942, just one of 35,000 Allied troops, he began his journey through Italy by train to the prisoner of war camps in Poland. From December 1942 to September 1943 he was imprisoned in the Italian P.O.W. Camp at Sforzacosta, awaiting transport north to Stalag VII A. Later, on 8 September 1943, about sixty miles north of Venice, a number of prisoners, Sid included, jumped from the moving train and escaped. For a time he hid in the small hospital of a Nunnery near to Costa Di Aviano, just south of the Alps. Moving on, Sid and three others were found hiding in a woodpile by an Italian family in the western part of Costa. The family led them to a chamber under the kitchen floor, where they hid from the Germans. It was a hiding place they would use many times. When the risk of discovery became too great, Sid left his hideout to protect the family. While in the mountains, he was captured again and sent to Stalag VII A. He would be moved to Stalag VIII B, near Lamsdorf later. When the Soviet armies advanced on Germany, the Germans decided to move the prisoners from the camps in Poland by marching them into Germany. In January and February 1945, two of the coldest winter months of the twentieth century, Sid, was one of thousands of allied prisoners, marched westward in groups of 200 to 300 in the so-called Death March (or Long March). Like most he was ill-prepared for the evacuation, having suffered years of poor rations and wearing clothing ill-suited to the appalling winter conditions. He marched up to 30 miles a day sleeping in broken barns, churches and more often than not under trees and hedges. There was no access to medical care and for much of the journey no food provided. He, along with his comrades, resorted to eating turnips they had to kick out of the frozen ground, leaves from the trees and on several occasions, grass. He also endured the brutality of the guards who had little incentive to keep the prisoners alive. Seeing one of his comrades struggling to keep up, Sid moved him in front so he could support and encourage him from behind. It was a decision that would trouble him throughout his later years as one particularly sadistic guard decided to arbitrarily single out prisoners to shoot by the roadside. One of those he selected was the comrade Sid had moved up in the line.

When freedom came, the Army reduced Sid's status from 'A1' to 'Class C' which rendered him unfit for active service and useful only for occupational work. After years of privation, he decided to pay a surprise visit to his parents in Haxey. When his mother opened the door, she did not recognise the emaciated 'stranger' on her doorstep!

Ralph Kitson of Epworth, a close friend of Sid, saw his period of captivity almost end when he, along with two other comrades, was selected to face a firing squad. When German guards came into their prison and marched them out, they lined them up in front of the white wall of a French cottage. As the guards began to pin white targets over their hearts, the three men feared the worst. The officer in charge, believed by many to be in a drunken stupor, paused the execution and insisted on all members of the

A Polish pocket watch Sid brought back from the war. He exchanged it with a starving Polish soldier for a loaf of bread.

village turning out to watch. As the German soldiers raised their rifles, several French women in the crowd lifted their aprons above their heads so as not to witness the punishment. Ralph closed his eyes and along with everyone else waited for the order to 'Fire!' It was an order that never came, as before he could deliver it, the inebriated officer fell to the ground seemingly incapable of giving the command. After a nervous few minutes, the soldiers lowered their rifles and laughing amongst themselves led the prisoners away, along with their, by now, unconscious officer!

Epworth's Dutch gabled Post Office, by Sid Sedgwick

St Andrew's Church, Epworth, by Sid Sedgwick

The Aegir Passes Down the Trent, by Sid Sedgwick

Looking down High Street, Epworth, by Sid Sedgwick

Printed in Great Britain
by Amazon